WEEKNIGHT KETO

75 QUICK & EASY RECIPES
FOR DELICIOUS LOW-CARB MEALS

WEEKNIGHT
KETO

KRISTY BERNARDO

Author of *Weeknight Cooking with Your Instant Pot*,
founder of The Wicked Noodle

Photography by BECKY WINKLER

PAGE STREET
PUBLISHING CO.

PAGE STREET
PUBLISHING CO.

Copyright © 2019 Kristy Bernardo

First published in 2019 by
Page Street Publishing Co.
27 Congress Street, Suite 105
Salem, MA 01970
www.pagestreetpublishing.com

Distributed by Macmillan, sales in Canada by The Canadian Manda Group.

23 22 21 20 19   1 2 3 4 5

ISBN-13: 978-1-62414-935-1
ISBN-10: 1-62414-935-9

Library of Congress Control Number: 2019941854

Cover and book design by Molly Gillespie for Page Street Publishing Co.
Photography © by Becky Winkler

Printed and bound in the United States

FOR ROB,
MY BEST FRIEND

TABLE OF CONTENTS

INTRODUCTION

Whenever the topic of the Keto lifestyle comes up in conversation, there are inevitably many questions. "How can you possibly give up bread? Pizza? There's no way I could ever do that!"

I thought the same thing, friends. To me, there's nothing better than a warm slice of bread, fresh from the oven, slathered with sea-salted butter. I never thought I could go without it, let alone enjoy the process.

But the Keto lifestyle has brought a lot of good things into my life. It's helped me keep my weight in check, the heartburn that plagued me almost 24 hours a day has disappeared and I just generally feel better.

My boyfriend Rob had an even better experience. In just six months, he dropped the 50 pounds (22.7 kg) he'd been struggling with for years. That was almost two years ago now and I doubt he'll ever go back to his carb-lovin' ways. He loves the Keto lifestyle even more than I do!

If you think you have to give up foods like pizza and fresh bread, I'm here to tell you that you don't. You won't have breads made with yeast and all-purpose flour, but there are many workarounds for this. A pizza made with a cauliflower crust is not only healthier, but you can still enjoy your favorite toppings! Such classic dishes as beef Stroganoff and lasagna taste just as delicious with cauliflower "rice" and zucchini "noodles." It may take a small amount of extra effort, but I promise you, the payoff will be huge.

I've intentionally created recipes for this book that are very simple, using as many mainstream and recognizable foods as possible. These recipes shouldn't feel like "Keto" recipes at all, but instead just delicious, easy recipes that happen to fall into the Keto lifestyle. My hope is that the recipes will make your Keto journey a simple one, which in turn will make it more enjoyable!

KBernardo

Delicious
30-MINUTE DINNERS

Speaking as a mom of two teenagers, my daily life gets pretty hectic. Those busy days and nights can make preparing a meal feel like a chore even for me, who passionately loves to cook! These recipes are my easy weeknight go-to meals. Many of them have portions that can be prepared ahead of time, too, making them almost as easy as opening a box and running the microwave.

MY 3 FAVORITES

Buffalo Chicken & Spinach–Stuffed Portobellos (page 12)

Taco-Stuffed Avocados (page 15)

Garlic Salmon in Foil (page 23)

BUFFALO CHICKEN & SPINACH-STUFFED PORTOBELLOS

With just five main ingredients, these flavorful portobellos come together with very little hands-on time and are a great way to use up leftover chicken. The earthy mushrooms and spinach combined with the spicy buffalo sauce make this meal a great weeknight treat! The leftovers reheat nicely for lunches the next day, too.

SERVES 4

4 portobello mushroom caps, stems removed and gills scraped off

1 tbsp (15 ml) avocado or extra virgin olive oil

2 cups (400 g) cooked, shredded chicken, at room temperature

2 cups (80 g) baby spinach leaves

¾ cup (84 g) mozzarella cheese, divided

½ cup (118 ml) Buffalo Sauce (page 177)

Coarse salt and freshly ground black pepper

Preheat your oven to 350°F (176°C).

Brush the mushrooms with avocado oil on both sides and place them on a sheet pan in one layer. Roast for about 12 minutes, or until they're mostly cooked through and have released their liquid. Remove from the oven, drain off the liquid and pat the mushrooms dry.

Meanwhile, in a medium-sized bowl, mix together the chicken, spinach, ½ cup (56 g) of the mozzarella cheese and the Buffalo sauce. Add salt and pepper to taste.

Fill the mushrooms evenly with the filling, then top them with the remaining cheese.

Place the mushrooms back in the oven and bake for another 15 minutes, or until the cheese is melted and the filling is heated through.

Note: If you're using cooked chicken that's been stored in the refrigerator and you're short on time, use it cold and simply add 5 minutes to your baking time.

Side Dish Recommendation:
roasted cauliflower or Cauliflower Rice (page 181)

Per serving: Calories: 365.9 kcal | Fat: 23.2 g | Carbs: 5.3 g | Fiber: 0.3 g | Protein: 34.6 g | Net Carbs: 5.0 g

TACO-STUFFED AVOCADOS

I like to make a double batch of this taco meat and enjoy it at a moment's notice all week long. The creamy avocado is well matched with the flavorful beef. I love that it's everything you'd get in a taco, just with a lot more heart-healthy avocado, making it the perfect choice for Keto followers. It's also super kid-friendly!

SERVES 4

2 lb (900 g) ground beef

3½ tbsp (28 g) Taco Seasoning (page 178)

1¼ cups (300 ml) water

1 (6-oz [170-g]) package baby spinach (optional)

4 avocados

1–2 cups (112–224 g) shredded Mexican-blend cheese

1 large tomato, chopped

In a large skillet, brown the ground beef over medium heat, 7 to 8 minutes. Drain off the fat.

Add the taco seasoning and water. Simmer, uncovered, until the mixture thickens slightly, 3 to 4 minutes.

If you're using spinach, divide it among 4 plates. Cut each avocado in half, remove the pit and remove each half in a solid piece from the skin, using a spoon. Place each avocado half on top of the spinach, then fill with some of the ground beef mixture (it will overflow). Top with the cheese and chopped tomato.

Serve immediately.

Side Dish Recommendation:
Rajas con Crema (Poblanos in Cream) (page 155)

Per serving: Calories: 986.3 kcal | Fat: 67.4 g | Carbs: 17.7 g | Fiber: 11.4 g | Protein: 79.1 g | Net Carbs: 6.2 g

CHEESY CRAB-STUFFED
PORTOBELLOS

I loved these cheesy, creamy stuffed portobellos long before I started my Keto lifestyle. The crab, garlic and cheeses combine to make a decadent, hearty dish. The filling can be made in advance, brought to room temperature, then baked on a busy weeknight.

SERVES 4

4 portobello mushrooms, stems and gills removed

1 tbsp (15 ml) avocado or extra virgin olive oil

8 oz (226 g) cream cheese, very soft

2 cloves garlic, minced

¼ cup (10 g) fresh parsley leaves, chopped

¼ cup (10 g) finely chopped green onions

¼ cup (28 g) shredded mozzarella cheese

½ cup (90 g) grated Parmesan cheese

½ tsp coarse salt

8 oz (226 g) fresh jumbo lump crabmeat

Preheat your oven to 375°F (190°C).

Brush the mushrooms with avocado oil on both sides and place them on a sheet pan in one layer. Roast for about 12 minutes. Remove from the oven, drain off all the liquid and pat the mushrooms dry.

In a medium-sized bowl, thoroughly mix the cream cheese, garlic, parsley, green onions, mozzarella cheese, Parmesan cheese and salt. Gently fold in the crabmeat.

Stuff the mushrooms evenly with the filling.

Place the mushrooms back in the oven and bake for 20 minutes, or until the filling is heated through and the mushrooms are cooked through.

Side Dish Recommendation:
Green Beans Almondine (page 143)

Per serving: Calories: 365 kcal | Fat: 28.8 g | Carbs: 5.6 g | Fiber: 0.5 g | Protein: 21.1 g | Net Carbs: 5.0 g

CHIMICHURRI RIB EYES

This chimichurri will become your new favorite Keto sauce! It's a snap to make, with ingredients you likely already have on hand. It pairs perfectly with rib eyes, but try it tossed with roasted cauliflower, too!

SERVES 4

FOR THE CHIMICHURRI SAUCE

1 cup (240 ml) extra virgin olive oil

2 cups (80 g) fresh flat-leaf parsley leaves

3 cloves garlic

¼ cup (10 g) fresh oregano leaves

¼ cup (60 ml) red wine vinegar

1 tsp coarse salt

1 tsp freshly ground black pepper

FOR THE STEAKS

4 rib-eye steaks (about 2 lb [900 g]), at room temperature

1 tbsp (15 ml) avocado oil (or any oil with a high smoke point, such as canola)

1 tsp coarse salt

1 tsp freshly ground black pepper

To make the chimichurri sauce, in a high-powered blender combine all the sauce ingredients and blend until smooth. Allow the sauce to sit at room temperature for at least 30 minutes for the flavors to meld.

To cook the steaks, heat a 12-inch (30-cm) cast-iron skillet over high heat until very hot, 5 to 6 minutes.

Brush the rib eyes with the avocado oil, then season both sides of the steaks with the salt and pepper.

Place the steaks in the hot skillet (you may have to work in batches; don't crowd the pan). Cook for 3 to 4 minutes, then flip the steaks and cook for another 3 minutes, or until they reach an internal temperature of 140°F (60°C) for medium-rare, or 155°F (68°C) for medium.

Transfer the steaks to a cutting board and let rest for 5 minutes. Slice the steaks against the grain and place on a serving platter. Top the steaks with the chimichurri sauce and serve. Extra chimichurri sauce can be served on the side.

Side Dish Recommendation:
roasted cauliflower or Cauliflower Rice (page 181)

Per serving: Calories: 1099.2 kcal | Fat: 92.0 g | Carbs: 4.6 g | Fiber: 2.0 g | Protein: 61.5 g | Net Carbs: 2.6 g

GRILLED CHICKEN
WITH PERUVIAN GREEN SAUCE

Our local Wegmans has a Peruvian green sauce that I've long used as a salad dressing. I started making it myself several years ago and was delighted when I realized it fits perfectly into my Keto diet. You'll be putting it on everything once you try it, and it pairs perfectly with grilled chicken!

SERVES 6

FOR THE MARINADE

1 tbsp (15 ml) avocado or extra virgin olive oil

1 cup (40 g) packed fresh cilantro leaves

1 clove garlic

2 jalapeño peppers, chopped

Juice of 1 small lime

⅓ cup (76 g) mayonnaise

½ tsp coarse salt

FOR THE CHICKEN

Juice of 1 lemon

3 tbsp (45 ml) avocado or extra virgin olive oil

2 cloves garlic, crushed

2 lb (900 g) boneless, skinless chicken breasts

To make the marinade, in a high-powered blender combine all the ingredients and blend until smooth. Cover tightly and allow the sauce to sit at room temperature for at least 30 minutes for the flavors to meld. Refrigerate if making in advance.

To prepare the chicken, place all the ingredients, including the marinade, in a ziplock bag and gently toss to coat. Marinate the chicken in the refrigerator for 30 to 60 minutes.

Discard the marinade. Preheat your grill over medium heat (375°F [190°C]) and grill the chicken breasts for about 6 minutes per side, or until cooked through to an internal temperature of 165°F (74°C).

Side Dish Recommendation:
Cauliflower Rice (page 181)

Per serving: Calories: 433.3 kcal | Fat: 25.9 g | Carbs: 1.7 g | Fiber: 0.3 g | Protein: 46.9 g | Net Carbs: 1.4 g

GARLIC SALMON IN FOIL

Salmon is so good for you and is a breeze to cook at home. Try this salmon as is, or put it over some greens for a delicious, healthy and filling salad. It's so simple yet so flavorful that you'll come back to this one often!

SERVES 6

3 tbsp (42 g) unsalted butter

Juice of 1 lemon

3 cloves garlic, minced

2 lb (900 g) salmon fillet, preferably wild-caught

1 tsp coarse salt

½ tsp freshly ground black pepper

Preheat your oven to 400°F (204°C).

In a small saucepan, combine the butter, lemon juice and garlic. Cook over low heat for 4 to 5 minutes, stirring frequently, until the butter is melted and the ingredients are well incorporated.

Place your salmon fillet on a piece of heavy-duty aluminum foil, large enough to fold over and cover it completely. Season the salmon with the salt and pepper.

Drizzle the garlic mixture over the salmon, then gently fold over the aluminum foil and crimp the edges to seal.

Place the foil-wrapped salmon on a sheet pan. Bake for about 15 minutes, or until cooked through to your liking.

Side Dish Recommendation:
Green Beans Almondine (page 143)

Per serving: Calories: 290.5 kcal | Fat: 14.2 g | Carbs: 1.1 g | Fiber: 0 g | Protein: 40.1 g | Net Carbs: 1.0 g

BOURSIN CHEESE & BACON-STUFFED CHICKEN BREASTS

Utilizing premade ingredients, such as Boursin cheese, adds a lot of flavor to a meal while keeping your prep to a minimum. These easy, cheesy chicken breasts come together quickly yet are delicious enough to serve to company.

SERVES 4

4 chicken breasts (about 2 lb [900 g] total)

1 tsp coarse salt

½ tsp freshly ground black pepper

1 (5.2-oz [150-g]) container Boursin cheese

8–12 slices bacon (not thick cut)

Preheat your oven to 400°F (204°C).

Make 5 or 6 slits crosswise in each chicken breast, about three-quarters of the way through the meat. Season the chicken with the salt and pepper.

Place a small amount of Boursin cheese into each slit, dividing it evenly among all the chicken breasts. Wrap each breast with 2 to 3 bacon slices, tucking the ends under the breasts so they don't curl up while baking.

Set an oven-safe rack on a sheet pan, then place the chicken breasts on the rack. Bake for 20 minutes, or until the chicken is cooked through to an internal temperature of 165°F (74°C).

If crispier bacon is desired after the chicken is fully cooked, place the chicken under the broiler for a few minutes.

Side Dish Recommendation:
grilled or roasted asparagus; Cauliflower Rice (page 181)

Per serving: Calories: 622.4 kcal | Fat: 31.4 g | Carbs: 1.6 g | Fiber: 0 g | Protein: 78.1 g | Net Carbs: 1.5 g

PARMESAN-CRUSTED CHICKEN & ASPARAGUS

I'll never go back to breading my chicken with anything but Parmesan! It forms a nice, golden crust and has wonderful flavor. You can even omit the almond flour if you don't have it on hand; simply increase the amount of Parmesan. The asparagus pairs nicely with the chicken, and it's a breeze because it's all roasted on the same pan!

SERVES 4

½ cup (90 g) grated Parmesan cheese

⅓ cup (32 g) almond flour

2 large eggs

4 boneless, skinless chicken breasts (about 2 lb [900 g])

1 tsp coarse salt, divided

½ tsp freshly ground black pepper, divided

1 lb (454 g) asparagus spears, washed and trimmed

2 tsp (10 ml) avocado or extra virgin olive oil

Preheat your oven to 350°F (176°C). Lightly spray an oven-safe rack with cooking spray.

In a small dish large enough to dredge the chicken, mix together the Parmesan cheese and almond flour. Gently beat the eggs in a separate, similarly sized dish.

Season the chicken breasts with ½ teaspoon of the salt and ¼ teaspoon of the pepper. Dredge each breast in the egg mixture, then in the flour mixture, making sure that each breast is entirely coated.

Place the breasts on the prepared rack and set on a sheet pan. Bake for 40 to 45 minutes, or until completely cooked through to an internal temperature of 165°F (74°C).

Toss the asparagus with the avocado oil, remaining ½ teaspoon of salt and ¼ teaspoon of pepper. During the last few minutes of cooking, place around the chicken on the rack and bake until crisp-tender, about 5 minutes.

Per serving: Calories: 581 kcal | Fat: 23.5 g | Carbs: 8.4 g | Fiber: 3.4 g | Protein: 81.3 g | Net Carbs: 4.9 g

BAKED GARLIC SHRIMP

Baking shrimp is the simplest way to cook it, and this recipe is my favorite to date. If you have the CarbQuik baking mix, try baking up a few biscuits for dipping in the sauce. Serve with a side salad to keep things in balance.

SERVES 4

½ cup (114 g) unsalted butter

3 cloves garlic, minced

2 lb (900 g) large shrimp, peeled and deveined (leave the tails on, if desired)

⅓ cup (13 g) fresh parsley leaves, chopped, divided

Juice and zest of 1 lemon

2 tbsp (30 ml) dry white wine

½ tsp coarse salt

¼ tsp freshly ground black pepper

Preheat your oven to 425°F (218°C).

In a small saucepan, melt the butter and garlic together over low heat, stirring frequently, about 5 minutes.

Place the shrimp in a large baking dish in one layer. Pour the butter mixture over the shrimp and sprinkle with all but 1 tablespoon (3 g) of the parsley. Toss gently to coat.

Bake for 3 minutes, then toss gently to flip the shrimp over. Bake for another 3 minutes, or until just cooked through.

Remove from the oven, add the lemon juice and zest, wine, salt and pepper and gently toss. Transfer the shrimp to a serving dish and garnish with the reserved parsley.

Side Dish Recommendation:
Cook some asparagus alongside the shrimp and it will all be done about the same time! Prepare the asparagus as instructed in the Parmesan-Crusted Chicken & Asparagus recipe (page 27). Place on a sheet pan next to the shrimp and bake until crisp-tender, about 5 minutes. It's also delicious with Creamy Broccoli with Pancetta & Pecorino (page 147).

Per serving: Calories: 442.5 kcal | Fat: 23.7 g | Carbs: 2.8 g | Fiber: 0.4 g | Protein: 55.0 g | Net Carbs: 2.4 g

CREAMY CHIPOTLE
CHICKEN BAKE

This is one of the first dishes I ever made when I began cooking fifteen years ago, and it remains one of our family's favorites. My mom made it for years before me; I just made it a touch more Keto-friendly.

SERVES 4

3 cloves garlic, chopped

2½ cups (600 ml) heavy cream

1 cup (240 ml) chicken broth

1 tsp chicken bouillon powder

3 chipotle peppers from a can of chipotles in adobo sauce

1 tbsp (15 ml) adobo sauce (from can of chipotle peppers)

2 tbsp (28 g) ghee, avocado oil or extra virgin olive oil

2 lb (900 g) boneless, skinless chicken breasts, cut into 1½" (4-cm) pieces

4 oz (114 g) cream cheese, cut into 8 pieces, at room temperature

In a high-powered blender, combine the garlic, cream, broth, bouillon, chipotle peppers and adobo sauce. Blend until very smooth. Set aside while you brown the chicken.

In a large skillet, heat the ghee over medium heat. Once it's shimmering, add the chicken. Cook the chicken for 5 to 6 minutes, turning once or twice, until browned and almost cooked through. Drain off any fat in the pan.

Add the chipotle mixture and cream cheese to the pan, gently stirring to coat the chicken. Gently simmer the sauce for about 5 minutes, or until it is hot, the cream cheese is well incorporated and the chicken is cooked through.

Side Dish Recommendation:
Cauliflower Rice (page 181); top it with some of the sauce!

Per serving: Calories: 717.2 kcal | Fat: 54.0 g | Carbs: 4.9 g | Fiber: 0.3 g | Protein: 52.0 g | Net Carbs: 4.6 g

CILANTRO CHICKEN PATTIES WITH AVOCADO

These chicken patties have a wonderful Mexican-like flavor and make a great Keto meal paired with heart-healthy avocado. They have a bit of spice from the jalapeños and pepper Jack cheese. Pair these with the Rajas con Crema (Poblanos in Cream) (page 155) for the perfect Keto meal!

SERVES 4

1 lb (454 g) ground chicken

½ cup (20 g) fresh cilantro

2 tsp (5 g) garlic powder

1 tbsp (14 g) chopped jalapeño peppers (fresh or pickled)

Juice of ½ lime

½ tsp coarse salt

½ tsp freshly ground black pepper

1 tbsp (15 ml) avocado or extra virgin olive oil

4 slices pepper Jack cheese

4 romaine lettuce leaves

1 small tomato, sliced

1 avocado, pitted, peeled and sliced

In a medium-sized bowl, mix together the chicken, cilantro, garlic powder, jalapeños, lime juice, salt and black pepper just until combined. Form into four 4-inch (10-cm)-diameter patties.

Heat a large skillet over medium heat. Add the avocado oil and, when it's shimmering, add the chicken patties. Cook until browned on both sides and cooked through completely, flipping once, about 10 minutes. Be careful not to overcook. The chicken patties should reach an internal temperature of 165°F (74°C).

Turn off the heat and top each patty with a slice of the cheese. Cover and let sit for about 5 minutes, or until the cheese is melted. Place each cheese-topped patty on a romaine leaf, then top with sliced tomato and avocado.

Side Dish Recommendation:
Rajas con Crema (Poblanos in Cream) (page 155)

Per serving: Calories: 399.3 kcal | Fat: 27.9 g | Carbs: 7.0 g | Fiber: 3.5 g | Protein: 32.5 g | Net Carbs: 3.5 g

FILET MIGNON WITH BLUE CHEESE BUTTER & ASPARAGUS

Filet mignon is always a treat, but paired with a creamy blue cheese butter, it's heaven! I love this recipe because it's quick and easy, plus the asparagus cooks at the same time that you're finishing the steaks in the oven.

SERVES 4

1 lb (454 g) thin asparagus spears, trimmed

1 tbsp + 1 tsp (20 ml) avocado oil, divided

1½ tsp (12 g) coarse salt, divided

½ cup (114 g [1 stick]) unsalted butter, softened

⅓ cup (37 g) crumbled blue cheese

4 (6-oz [168-g]) filet mignon steaks, at room temperature

2 tbsp (16 g) coarsely ground black pepper

Preheat your oven to 400°F (204°C).

On a plate, toss the asparagus with 1 teaspoon of the avocado oil and ½ teaspoon of the salt, then set aside.

In a small bowl, use a spoon or fork to mix together the butter and blue cheese, then set aside.

Season the steaks with the remaining salt and pepper.

Heat a large cast-iron skillet over high heat. Add the remaining tablespoon (15 ml) of avocado oil and, when it's shimmering, add the steaks. Sear the steaks for about 2 minutes per side, until both sides are nicely browned.

Place the asparagus on top of the steaks, then place the skillet in the oven. Alternatively, you can also place the asparagus on a separate sheet pan if your skillet isn't large enough. Bake for 4 to 5 minutes, or until the steaks are done to your likeness and the asparagus is crisp-tender. You can use a meat thermometer to test for doneness; 125°F (52°C) for medium-rare is recommended.

Top each steak with some of the blue cheese butter.

Per serving: Calories: 456.6 kcal | Fat: 40.3 g | Carbs: 7.1 g | Fiber: 3.3 g | Protein: 18.8 g | Net Carbs: 3.8 g

Classic CARB FAVORITES MADE KETO

Oh how I love enjoying my favorite comfort foods Keto style. They're what everyone misses most when first starting their Keto journey. I certainly did! So, I made sure to create these so that you never have to feel like you are missing out. Serve these to non-Keto followers and they usually can't even tell it's Keto! This chapter is filled with my favorites, and probably yours, too! Pizza, fried chicken, mac and cheese . . . and all so delicious that you'll never miss the carbs.

MY 3 FAVORITES
Pickle-Brined Fried Chicken (page 38)
Ground Beef Stroganoff (page 58)
Lemon-Pepper Chicken Wings (page 61)

PICKLE-BRINED FRIED CHICKEN

I'll never forget the look on Rob's face the first time he tasted this chicken. He was convinced it couldn't be Keto! I highly recommend using whey protein isolate as a breading. I'm not big on specialty ingredients, and it may sound strange, but it creates the perfect crust and tastes amazing! If you like spicy chicken, try using the juice from a jar of jalapeño pickles.

SERVES 6

3 lb (1.3 kg) boneless, skinless chicken thighs

2 cups (480 ml) pickle juice (from a jar of pickles)

2 large eggs, beaten

1 heaping tbsp (14 g) mayonnaise

1 tsp Dijon mustard

½ tsp coarse salt

¼ tsp freshly ground black pepper

2 cups (480 ml) avocado oil

2 cups (80 g) whey protein isolate or finely crushed pork rinds

Place the chicken in a large ziplock bag. Pour the pickle juice over the chicken and place the bag in the refrigerator. Marinate for 8 to 24 hours, depending on how much pickle flavor you want your chicken to have. I go for the full 24!

Drain the chicken and discard the pickle juice. Pat the chicken dry with paper towels and cut into 2 or 3 pieces each, if desired.

In a medium-sized bowl, mix together the eggs, mayo, Dijon, salt and pepper, then toss the chicken in the mixture, taking care that it's entirely coated.

In a large, deep skillet, heat the avocado oil over medium heat until shimmering. Working quickly, dredge each piece of chicken in the whey protein (or pork rinds) and place it in the oil. Work in batches if necessary. Cook until both sides are well browned and the chicken is cooked through, turning just once, 3 to 4 minutes.

Drain the cooked chicken of excess oil and place on paper towels. Serve with your favorite sauce.

Side Dish Recommendation:
Chipotle Cauliflower "Potato" Salad (page 148)

Per serving: Calories: 611.3 kcal | Fat: 34.7 g | Carbs: 1.4 g |
Fiber: 0.1 g | Protein: 72.7 g | Net Carbs: 1.3 g

CAJUN CHICKEN ALFREDO

I've tried just about everything to duplicate pasta, and hearts of palm is the closest thing I've found. You really—really!—will think you're eating "real" pasta. The best part is that it comes in cans, so it's ready to serve anytime. My local grocer carries these, but if you have trouble finding them, Amazon is a good source. Of course, you can also use zucchini noodles ("zoodles") or just put the sauce over cauliflower rice or florets.

SERVES 4

2 lb (900 g) boneless, skinless chicken breasts, cut into 1" (2.5-cm) pieces

1½ tsp (12 g) coarse salt, divided

1 tbsp (15 ml) avocado or extra virgin olive oil

2 cloves garlic, minced

1 tbsp (8 g) Cajun Seasoning (page 180)

3 tbsp (42 g) unsalted butter

2 cups (480 ml) heavy cream

1 cup (180 g) grated Parmesan cheese

½ tsp freshly ground black pepper

2 tbsp (5 g) chopped fresh parsley

1 (14-oz [400-g]) can hearts of palm linguine or fettuccine, rinsed, well drained and gently patted dry (such as Palmini brand)

Season the chicken breasts with ½ teaspoon of the salt.

Heat a large skillet over medium heat. Add the avocado oil and, when it's shimmering, add the chicken. Cook until the chicken is lightly browned, about 5 minutes.

Add the garlic, Cajun seasoning and butter to the pan. Cook for about 1 minute, stirring frequently.

Add the cream to the pan and bring to a simmer. Cook, stirring frequently, until the chicken is cooked through, about 5 more minutes. Stir in the cheese; continue to cook, stirring, until it's fully incorporated. Add the remaining teaspoon of salt and the pepper; taste the sauce and add more salt if necessary.

Remove from the heat and stir in the parsley and hearts of palm "noodles." Serve immediately.

Per serving: Calories: 722.7 kcal | Fat: 50.0 g | Carbs: 7.4 g | Fiber: 2.0 g | Protein: 59.9 g | Net Carbs: 5.4 g

ZUCCHINI CHEESE PIZZA

I make this easy pizza at least weekly. I highly recommend making a big bowl of shredded zucchini to use in recipes for the week. If you squeeze the water out before storing, it will last much longer, too! Then simply take out a couple of cups and have this delicious pizza any ol' time.

SERVES 2

2 cups (400 g) packed shredded zucchini

½ tsp coarse salt

1 large egg

¼ cup (24 g) finely ground almond flour

¼ tsp Italian seasoning

1 cup (112 g) shredded mozzarella cheese, divided

⅓ cup (60 g) grated Parmesan cheese

Preheat your oven to 425°F (218°C).

Start by making the zucchini crust. Place the zucchini in a large colander. Sprinkle with the salt and let the zucchini sit for 10 minutes so some of its water is released.

Working in batches (don't overstuff), press the zucchini in a potato ricer to remove as much water as possible. Alternatively, you can use a kitchen towel for this, although I've found that a ricer is the best tool for the job.

In a medium-sized bowl, mix together the zucchini, egg, flour, Italian seasoning and ¼ cup (28 g) of the mozzarella.

Place the zucchini mixture on a sheet pan lined with a sheet of parchment paper. Gently spread the mixture into a circle until it's very thin, about ¼ inch (6 mm) thick.

Bake for 15 to 20 minutes, or until the edges are gently browned. Remove from the oven and carefully remove the crust, flipping it over onto the same sheet of parchment paper. Sprinkle with the remaining ¾ cup (84 g) of mozzarella, then the Parmesan cheese. Bake for another 10 minutes, or until the cheese is melted and starting to brown.

Note: Try adding some pepperoni on top of the cheese after you flip the crust!

Side Dish Recommendation:
Bacon-Wrapped Brussels Sprouts with Maple Syrup (page 144)

Per serving: Calories: 194 kcal | Fat: 14.3 g | Carbs: 5.3 g | Fiber: 1.3 g | Protein: 12.2 g | Net Carbs: 3.9 g

BUFFALO ROASTED CAULIFLOWER "NACHOS"

Don't let the name fool you: These "nachos" are more of a hearty dinner than an appetizer. I make this for football games when the Packers play, to bring us good luck. They're so flavorful and everyone loves them!

SERVES 6

1 head cauliflower, stem and leaves discarded, cut into small florets

¾ cup (180 ml) Ranch Dressing (page 176), divided

¼ cup (45 g) grated Parmesan cheese

¼ cup (45 g) finely crushed pork rinds

1 rotisserie chicken, meat removed and shredded

½ cup (118 ml) Buffalo Sauce (page 177)

¼ cup (10 g) chopped green onions

¼ cup (28 g) crumbled blue cheese

Preheat your oven to 400°F (204°C).

In a bowl, toss the cauliflower florets with ½ cup (118 ml) of ranch dressing. In a separate bowl, mix together the Parmesan cheese and pork rinds. Place the coated cauliflower in a large ziplock bag and add the cheese mixture. Shake and toss to coat the cauliflower completely.

Place the cauliflower in a single layer on a large sheet pan lined with parchment paper. Roast in the oven for 20 minutes. Toss the cauliflower, then roast for 20 minutes more, or until well browned; it's okay if some of the tiny pieces get very brown—those little bits are the best part!

Top the cauliflower with the shredded chicken. Drizzle with the Buffalo sauce and the remaining ranch dressing and sprinkle with the green onions and blue cheese. Serve immediately.

Per serving: Calories: 547.1 kcal | Fat: 33.4 g | Carbs: 5.5 g | Fiber: 2.4 g | Protein: 54.8 g | Net Carbs: 3.1 g

COTTAGE PIE

This is what I make when I know I'll have a busy workweek and want lots of leftovers. It's one of those dishes that gets better with time and it's very filling! To make this Keto, I top it with a buttery, Parmesan-crusted cauliflower topping instead of potatoes, as well as cut back on the tomato paste and red wine to keep the carbs in check.

SERVES 6

4 cups (680 g) cauliflower florets

3 tbsp (24 g) unsalted butter, at room temperature, divided

2 large egg yolks

¼ cup (60 ml) heavy cream

2 tsp (16 g) coarse salt, divided

2 lb (900 g) ground beef

½ medium-sized onion, chopped

8 oz (224 g) sliced mushrooms

8 oz (224 g) green beans, trimmed and cut into ½" (1.3-cm) pieces

3 cloves garlic, minced

1 tsp dried thyme

2 tbsp (28 g) tomato paste

½ cup (118 ml) red wine

2 cups (480 ml) beef stock or broth

1 tbsp (15 ml) Worcestershire sauce

½ tsp freshly ground black pepper

½ cup (90 g) grated Parmesan cheese

Preheat your oven to 375°F (190°C).

Place the cauliflower in a steamer basket set inside a pot of boiling water, then cover the pot. Cook until the cauliflower is very tender, 8 to 10 minutes. Drain the cauliflower and allow it to cool until warm and cool enough to handle.

Transfer the cauliflower to a large mixing bowl. Add 2 tablespoons (16 g) of the butter, plus the egg yolks and cream. Using an immersion blender, puree the cauliflower mixture until smooth. Alternatively, you can use a potato masher if you like a chunkier consistency. Add 1 teaspoon of the coarse salt and stir well to incorporate. Set aside while you make the pie.

In a large, oven-safe skillet, brown the ground beef over medium heat until no pink remains, 7 to 8 minutes. Remove with a slotted spoon and set aside. Drain the fat from the pan.

Add the onion, mushrooms and green beans to the skillet and cook for 4 to 5 minutes, or until the onion is soft. Add the garlic and thyme and cook, stirring frequently, for 1 minute more. Stir in the tomato paste. Whisk in the wine, beef stock and Worcestershire until smooth. Return the beef to the pan and season it with the remaining teaspoon of salt and the pepper.

Carefully spread the mashed cauliflower over the beef mixture, taking care to cover it completely. Melt the remaining 1 tablespoon (8 g) of butter, then drizzle it over the mashed cauliflower and sprinkle with the Parmesan.

Bake for 30 minutes, or until the filling is bubbling and the top is browned. Place under the broiler for an additional few minutes, if necessary.

Remove from the oven and allow to rest for 10 minutes before serving.

Per serving: Calories: 401.3 kcal | Fat: 23.1 g | Carbs: 9.6 g | Fiber: 2.9 g | Protein: 36.0 g | Net Carbs: 6.3 g

CAULIFLOWER "MAC" & CHEESE

My favorite comfort food has always been mac and cheese. This easy, creamy, cheesy dish makes me forget I'm Keto and just makes me happy! You'll never believe it's not the real deal.

SERVES 4

1 head cauliflower, cut into small florets

1 tbsp (15 ml) avocado or extra virgin olive oil

1 tsp coarse salt, divided

½ cup (90 g) grated Parmesan cheese, divided

1 cup (240 ml) heavy cream

⅓ cup (150 g) cream cheese, at room temperature

1 tsp Dijon mustard

2½ cups (280 g) shredded cheddar cheese, divided

Cooking spray

Preheat your oven to 425°F (218°C).

On a sheet pan, toss the cauliflower florets with the avocado oil and ½ teaspoon of the salt.

Roast for about 45 minutes, tossing every 15 minutes, until soft and lightly browned. Toss with ¼ cup (45 g) of the Parmesan cheese and roast for another 5 minutes.

In a large saucepan, heat the cream over medium heat until gently bubbling. Add the cream cheese, mustard, remaining ¼ cup (45 g) of Parmesan, 1½ cups (168 g) of the cheddar cheese and the remaining ½ teaspoon of salt, stirring until smooth. Add the cauliflower and gently toss it to coat.

Spray an 8-inch (20-cm) square baking dish with cooking spray and pour the mixture into it. Top with the remaining 1 cup (112 g) of cheddar cheese. Bake for 15 to 20 minutes, or until bubbling hot and the cheese is starting to brown. Remove from the oven and allow to sit for about 5 minutes before serving.

Side Dish Recommendation:
Green Beans Almondine (page 143)

Per serving: Calories: 470.2 kcal | Fat: 41.8 g | Carbs: 8.3 g | Fiber: 2.2 g | Protein: 16.8 g | Net Carbs: 6.1 g

STUFFED PEPPERS

Stuffed peppers is a dish my mom made while I was growing up, and I still love it to this day. Cauliflower rice makes a wonderful substitute for real rice—I can't even tell the difference! This is a wonderful cold-weather meal that will make your home smell heavenly.

SERVES 6

FOR THE FILLING

1 tsp avocado or extra virgin olive oil

½ large onion, chopped

3 cloves garlic, minced

1½ lb (675 g) ground beef

¾ cup (138 g) cooked Cauliflower Rice (page 181)

10 oz (283 ml) Tomato Sauce (page 182)

1 tbsp (15 ml) Worcestershire sauce

Kosher salt and freshly ground black pepper

FOR THE SAUCE

1 tbsp (15 ml) extra virgin olive oil

1 medium-sized onion, chopped

1 tsp dried basil

1 tsp dried oregano

3 cloves garlic, minced

1 tbsp (16 g) tomato paste

1 (28-oz [794-g]) can petite-diced tomatoes

½ tsp kosher salt

¼ tsp freshly ground black pepper

FOR ASSEMBLY

6 large red bell peppers (or your favorite color)

1 cup (112 g) shredded mozzarella cheese

¼ cup (10 g) chopped fresh parsley

Preheat your oven to 350°F (176°C).

To make the filling, heat a large skillet over medium heat. Add the avocado oil and, when it's shimmering, add the onion and cook for about 5 minutes, stirring occasionally, until soft. Add the garlic and cook for 1 minute more. Add the ground beef and cook until browned and no pink remains, 7 to 8 minutes. Drain off any fat, then add the cauliflower rice, tomato sauce and Worcestershire. Cook a few more minutes until the mixture is hot, then add the salt and black pepper to taste.

To make the sauce, heat a skillet over medium heat and add the olive oil. Add the onion and sauté, stirring occasionally, for about 5 minutes or until soft. Add the basil, oregano and garlic and cook for 1 to 2 minutes more. Stir in the tomato paste and cook for an additional 2 to 3 minutes. Add the diced tomatoes, salt and pepper, stir well and bring to a simmer. Allow to simmer, stirring occasionally, for another 10 minutes.

To assemble, cut off the tops of the bell peppers and remove the seeds and membranes. Slice a small amount off the bottom of each pepper, if necessary, to make each stand upright. Place the peppers in a baking dish just large enough to fit them all upright. Spoon the filling into the peppers, mounding it over the top. Spoon the sauce over the top of each pepper, allowing the excess to fall over the sides. Cover and bake for 45 minutes.

Remove the cover and top each pepper with the shredded cheese. Place back in the oven and bake, uncovered, for another 15 minutes, or until the cheese is melted and gooey and the peppers are soft and cooked through. Sprinkle with the parsley and serve.

Per serving: Calories: 264.8 kcal | Fat: 15.6 g | Carbs: 9.9 g | Fiber: 1.5 g | Protein: 21.4 g | Net Carbs: 8.4 g

---

ITALIAN SAUSAGE BURGERS & GARLIC SPINACH

The garlic spinach and the Italian sausage pair perfectly in this dish. I love using spinach in lieu of a carb-laden bun, and you will, too! Try this method for all of your burgers for a filling, healthy Keto meal.

SERVES 4

1 lb (454 g) ground Italian sausage

1 tbsp (15 ml) avocado or extra virgin olive oil

2 cloves garlic, minced

1 (10-oz [283-g]) bag baby spinach

¼ tsp coarse salt

¼ tsp freshly ground black pepper

4 slices fresh mozzarella

4 slices tomato

¼ cup (56 g) Basil Pesto (page 184)

Form the Italian sausage meat into four 4-inch (10-cm)-diameter patties and set aside.

Heat a large skillet over medium heat. Add the avocado oil and, when it's shimmering, add the garlic. Cook for 1 minute, stirring frequently. Add the spinach and cook until it's wilted, 2 to 3 minutes. Season with the salt and pepper. Remove the spinach and set aside.

Add the sausage patties and cook for about 5 minutes, or until nicely browned on the bottom. Flip the burgers and cook for another 4 to 5 minutes, or until the other side is browned and each burger is cooked through (160°F [71°C]). Turn off the heat and top each burger with 1 slice each of mozzarella and tomato. Cover the pan and allow the cheese and tomato to soften, about 5 more minutes.

Divide the spinach among 4 serving plates and top each with 1 burger. Top each burger with 1 tablespoon (14 g) of the pesto and serve.

Side Dish Recommendation:
Chipotle Cauliflower "Potato" Salad (page 148)

Per serving: Calories: 591.2 kcal | Fat: 47.6 g | Carbs: 9.1 g | Fiber: 2.0 g | Protein: 30.4 g | Net Carbs: 7.1 g

BACON JAM CHEESEBURGERS

The only thing better than a cheeseburger is one topped with bacon jam! Make a few extra burgers for reheating during the week to save you time and to keep your belly happy.

SERVES 4

1½ lb (675 g) ground beef

2 cloves garlic, minced

½ tsp Worcestershire sauce

½ tsp coarse kosher salt

¼ tsp freshly ground black pepper

2 tsp (10 ml) avocado or extra virgin olive oil

4 slices sharp cheddar cheese

4 romaine lettuce leaves

1 medium-sized tomato, sliced

¾ cup (170 g) Bacon Jam (page 156), at room temperature

In a medium-sized bowl, mix together the ground beef, garlic, Worcestershire, salt and pepper. Form into four 5-inch (12.5-cm)-diameter patties.

Heat a large skillet over medium heat. Add the avocado oil and, when it's shimmering, add the beef patties. Cook the burgers for about 5 minutes per side, or until done to your liking (medium-rare is recommended).

Turn off the heat, top each burger with a slice of the cheese and cover until melted, about 2 minutes.

Place each burger on a serving plate and top with a lettuce leaf, sliced tomato and bacon jam.

Side Dish Recommendation:
Chipotle Cauliflower "Potato" Salad (page 148)

Per serving: Calories: 849.3 kcal | Fat: 54.9 g | Carbs: 8.0 g | Fiber: 2.0 g | Protein: 76.5 g | Sugar Alcohols: 1.2 g | Net Carbs: 4.8 g

---

SPICY CHICKEN & AVOCADO TACOS

Crunchy romaine lettuce is a good alternative to tortillas. We've also picked up low-carb tortillas and they work well, too. This recipe is filling and so flavorful, your non-Keto friends will be jealous.

SERVES 4

1 lb (454 g) boneless, skinless chicken breasts, cut into 1" (2.5-cm) pieces

1 tbsp (15 ml) avocado or extra virgin olive oil

1 tbsp (8 g) Taco Seasoning (page 178)

½ cup (115 g) sour cream

1 tbsp (15 ml) adobo sauce (from a can of chipotle peppers)

4 romaine lettuce leaves

1 avocado, sliced

1 small tomato, chopped

2 tbsp (5 g) chopped fresh cilantro

In a medium-sized bowl, toss the chicken with the avocado oil and taco seasoning and set aside for about 20 minutes.

In a small bowl, mix together the sour cream and adobo sauce, then set aside.

Heat a large skillet over medium heat. Add the chicken and cook until browned on all sides and cooked through, 7 to 8 minutes.

Fill each lettuce leaf with one-quarter of the chicken mixture, then top it with sliced avocado, tomato, cilantro and the adobo sour cream.

Side Dish Recommendation:
Rajas con Crema (Poblanos in Cream) (page 155)

Per serving: Calories: 356.8 kcal | Fat: 19.7 g | Carbs: 7.2 g | Fiber: 3.9 g | Protein: 37.2 g | Net Carbs: 3.3 g

GROUND BEEF STROGANOFF

This easy stroganoff recipe is a comfort food staple. It's creamy and rich, and I've even served it over raw spinach to make a healthy, warm salad! You may omit the brandy if you wish, but it adds a depth of flavor that we love. I serve this over cauliflower rice, but zucchini noodles ("zoodles") are also delicious.

SERVES 6

1 tbsp (15 ml) ghee or avocado oil

1 lb (454 g) cremini mushrooms, sliced

1½ lb (675 g) ground beef

¼ onion, chopped

1 clove garlic, minced

2 tsp (10 ml) Worcestershire sauce

1 tbsp (15 ml) brandy

½ cup (118 ml) beef broth

½ cup (115 g) sour cream

¼ cup (60 ml) heavy cream

½ tsp coarse salt

½ tsp freshly ground black pepper

¼ cup (10 g) chopped fresh chives

6 cups (678 g) cooked Cauliflower Rice (page 181)

Heat a large skillet over high heat. Add the ghee and, when it's shimmering, add the mushrooms. Cook until they've released their liquid and it has evaporated, then allow the mushrooms to brown, about 8 minutes. Remove the mushrooms with a slotted spoon and set aside.

Lower the heat to medium and add the ground beef to the pan. Cook until almost no pink remains, 7 to 8 minutes, then drain off the fat. Add the onion and cook, stirring occasionally, for 3 to 4 minutes. Add the garlic and cook, stirring frequently, for 1 minute more.

Add the Worcestershire, brandy, beef broth, sour cream, cream, salt and pepper to the pan. Stir just until heated through and the sauce is smooth. Top with the chives and serve over the cauliflower rice.

Note: If the sauce is too thick for your liking, add a little more beef broth before removing from the heat.

Per serving: Calories: 448.7 kcal | Fat: 29.9 g | Carbs: 6.5 g | Fiber: 1.8 g | Protein: 34.2 g | Net Carbs: 4.4 g

LEMON-PEPPER CHICKEN WINGS

If any recipe is my go-to for any day of the week, it's this one. My dad always asks me to make these wings for him, and my girls love them, too. Perfect for a party or just an easy, weeknight meal with a salad, you'll love having almost no prep time.

SERVES 4

4 lb (1.8 kg) chicken wings, washed and patted dry

¼ cup (60 ml) avocado oil (or another oil with a high smoke point)

¼ cup (57 g [½ stick]) unsalted butter, melted

2 tbsp (25 g) Lemon-Pepper Seasoning (page 179)

Preheat your oven to 400°F (204°C).

In a large bowl, toss the wings with the avocado oil until completely coated.

Place the wings on an oven-safe rack set on a sheet pan. Bake for 50 to 60 minutes, or until the wings are cooked through and their skin is crispy.

In a small bowl, mix together the melted butter and lemon-pepper seasoning. Using a basting brush, coat the wings with the butter mixture. Serve immediately.

Note: *If making ahead, bake as normal, then recrisp them under the broiler for a few minutes until hot.*

Side Dish Recommendation:
Twice-Baked Mashed Parmesan Cauliflower (page 139)

Per serving: Calories: 690.9 kcal | Fat: 50.9 g | Carbs: 0.9 g | Fiber: 0.2 g | Protein: 54.1 g | Net Carbs: 0.7 g

Light & Fresh
KETO DISHES

One of the things I struggled the most with when I began my Keto journey was lunch. Breakfast was simple: two soft-boiled eggs sprinkled with a little truffle salt and a few slices of prosciutto. Dinner was always planned because I'm in charge of feeding this family of mine. But around lunchtime, I was busy working, and stopping to make a light, Keto-friendly meal just for myself was too time consuming.

The recipes in this chapter are perfect for lunch or dinner. The Zucchini Noodle Lasagna (page 64) makes wonderful leftovers for lunches, and the shrimp salad in the Shrimp Salad & Avocado Lettuce Wraps (page 71) can be made ahead of time so you can enjoy it all week long. Be sure to try Creamy Chipotle Asparagus Scrambled Eggs (page 75), too! I've been making them for years, long before Keto came into my life. You'll love all of these recipes and will feel great eating them, too!

MY 3 FAVORITES
Chimichurri Chicken Bites (page 68)
Shrimp Salad & Avocado Lettuce Wraps (page 71)
Creamy Chipotle Asparagus Scrambled Eggs (page 75)

ZUCCHINI NOODLE LASAGNA

Zucchini as pasta is one of my favorite Keto swaps. I add eggplant to this dish for another layer of flavor. Serve with a side salad and indulge with a nice glass of Keto-friendly wine, such as cabernet or chardonnay.

SERVES 8

2 medium-sized zucchini, sliced lengthwise into thin slices (6–8 slices each)

2 small eggplants, sliced crosswise into thin slices (6–8 slices each)

1 tbsp + 1 tsp (32 g) coarse salt, divided

1 cup (230 g) whole-milk ricotta cheese

1 large egg

½ cup (90 g) grated Parmesan cheese

½ cup (113 g) Basil Pesto (page 184)

1 batch (about 25 oz [709 g]) Marinara Sauce (page 183)

2 cups (224 g) shredded whole-milk mozzarella cheese

2 tbsp (5 g) fresh basil leaves, chopped

Preheat your oven to 375°F (190°C).

Place the zucchini and eggplant slices on a large cutting board and sprinkle with 1 tablespoon (24 g) of the salt. Allow the zucchini and eggplant to sit for 20 to 30 minutes so they release some water. Wipe away the water and salt with a paper towel.

In a small bowl, mix together the ricotta cheese, egg, Parmesan cheese, pesto and the remaining teaspoon of salt until smooth.

Grease a 7-inch (18-cm) round baking pan. Place a thin layer of marinara sauce on the bottom of the pan. Top with one layer each of half of the zucchini, eggplant and the ricotta mixture, then a layer of shredded mozzarella. Layer once more, adding another layer of sauce as you go, ending with a final layer of just sauce and the mozzarella (I like to make my top layer of cheese the thickest).

Cover your pan with aluminum foil and bake the lasagna for 30 minutes. Remove the foil and bake for another 5 to 10 minutes, or until the cheese is bubbling hot and lightly browned on the top.

Sprinkle with fresh basil and serve.

Note: If you'd prefer to reduce the carbs in this recipe, you can omit the eggplant entirely, or replace it with more zucchini.

Per serving: Calories: 454.5 kcal | Fat: 35.1 g | Total Carbs: 12.4 g | Fiber: 3.1 g | Protein: 23.0 g | Net Carbs: 9.2 g

CAULIFLOWER-CRUST CAPRESE PIZZA

There's a local pizzeria where I live that serves a cauliflower-crust pizza. I tried it long before I was Keto, and I was hooked! Be sure to keep the crust thin for the best results. The garlic, basil and cheeses make this pizza a flavor-filled Italian treat!

SERVES 2

1 head cauliflower, broken into florets

1 large egg

3 cloves garlic, minced

¼ cup (10 g) chopped fresh basil, divided

1 tbsp (3 g) chopped flat-leaf parsley

1 tsp coarse salt

½ tsp freshly ground black pepper

½ cup (56 g) shredded mozzarella cheese

¼ cup (45 g) grated Parmesan cheese

1 (8-oz ([226-g]) ball fresh mozzarella, sliced

1 medium-sized tomato, sliced

Preheat your oven to 425°F (218°C).

Using a food processor, pulse the cauliflower until it turns into "rice." In a medium-sized bowl, stir together the cauliflower and egg until combined. Add the garlic, 1 tablespoon (3 g) of the basil, parsley, salt, pepper, shredded mozzarella cheese and Parmesan cheese; stir until just combined.

Place the cauliflower mixture on a sheet pan lined with parchment paper. Press into a thin circle about ¼ inch (6 mm) thick.

Bake for about 10 minutes, or until the edges are beginning to brown.

Remove the pizza from the oven and top it with the fresh mozzarella slices and the sliced tomato. Bake for another 5 to 7 minutes, or just until the mozzarella and tomatoes are soft.

Sprinkle with the remaining 3 tablespoons (7 g) of basil and serve.

Side Dish Recommendation:
Roasted or grilled asparagus

Per serving: Calories: 314.2 kcal | Fat: 21.3 g | Carbs: 9.9 g |
Fiber: 3.8 g | Protein: 22.5 g | Net Carbs: 6.1 g

CHIMICHURRI CHICKEN BITES

Chimichurri sauce is one of my staples for the Keto diet. It has a wonderful tang and is a great way to get your fat macros up. The sauce is great over plain chicken or fish, but once you try it with these flavorful chicken bites, you might not want to try it any other way! It also makes a wonderful party appetizer. Just add toothpicks for your guests and serve these on a pretty platter so everyone can see the bright green color of the sauce.

SERVES 4

FOR THE CHIMICHURRI SAUCE

2 cups (80 g) fresh parsley

¼ cup (10 g) fresh oregano

3 cloves garlic

¼ cup (60 ml) red wine vinegar

1 cup (240 ml) avocado oil

½ tsp red pepper flakes

½ tsp coarse salt

½ tsp freshly ground black pepper

FOR THE CHICKEN BITES

2 lb (900 g) ground chicken

2 large eggs

3 cloves garlic, minced

½ cup (90 g) finely crushed pork rinds

1 tsp coarse salt

½ tsp freshly ground black pepper

2 tbsp (30 ml) avocado oil

To make the chimichurri sauce, in a high-powered blender, combine all the sauce ingredients and blend until smooth. Allow the sauce to sit at room temperature while you make the chicken bites, to allow the flavors to meld.

To make the chicken bites, in a medium-sized bowl use your hands to mix together the ground chicken, eggs, garlic, pork rinds, salt and pepper. Form the mixture into bite-size balls, about 1 inch (2.5 cm) in diameter.

In a large skillet, heat the avocado oil over medium-high heat. Add the chicken bites and cook until they're nicely browned on all sides and cooked through, 7 to 8 minutes.

Pour some of the sauce into a serving dish and place the chicken bites on top of the sauce. Serve the remaining sauce on the side for dipping.

Side Dish Recommendation:
roasted cauliflower or Cauliflower Rice (page 181)

Per serving: Calories: 543 kcal | Fat: 36.0 g | Carbs: 6.0 g | Fiber: 2.0 g | Protein: 49.0 g | Net Carbs: 4.0 g

SHRIMP SALAD & AVOCADO
LETTUCE WRAPS

These delicious wraps are the perfect summer meal! I'll take them to outdoor concerts and assemble them there, or make them throughout the week for an easy lunch.

SERVES 4

3 lb (1.3 kg) cooked shrimp, chopped

Juice of 1 lemon

1 celery stalk, finely chopped

2 green onions, chopped

1 cup (230 g) mayonnaise

1 tsp coarse salt, divided

¼ tsp freshly ground black pepper

8 romaine lettuce leaves

2 avocados, sliced

1 medium-sized tomato, sliced

In a medium-sized bowl, mix together the shrimp, lemon juice, celery, green onions, mayonnaise, ½ teaspoon of the salt and the pepper. Refrigerate for at least 1 hour to allow the flavors to meld.

Place the lettuce leaves on 4 individual serving plates, then top each with the shrimp salad, dividing it evenly. Top with the avocado and tomato slices, then season with the remaining ½ teaspoon of salt. Serve immediately.

Side Dish Recommendation:
Bacon Broccoli Cheese Bites (page 151)

Per serving: Calories: 412.8 kcal | Fat: 25.3 g | Carbs: 5.8 g | Fiber: 3.4 g | Protein: 42.3 g | Net Carbs: 2.4 g

SALMON CAKES WITH LEMON-DIJON AIOLI

I keep cans of salmon on hand so I can make this recipe at the last minute. It uses ingredients that I almost always have in the refrigerator, plus it comes together so quickly.

SERVES 3

FOR THE AIOLI

¾ cup (174 g) mayonnaise

¼ cup (58 g) Dijon mustard

2 cloves garlic, minced

Juice of 1 lemon

½ tsp coarse salt

FOR THE SALMON CAKES

1 (4.75-oz [418-g]) can salmon

1 large egg

½ cup (115 g) mayonnaise

½ cup (45 g) finely crushed pork rinds

¼ tsp garlic powder

Coarse salt, to taste

¼ tsp freshly ground black pepper

2 tsp (10 ml) avocado oil or extra virgin olive oil

OPTIONAL TOPPINGS

Sliced tomato and/or avocado

To make the aioli, in a small bowl mix all the aioli ingredients together. Cover and refrigerate for at least 1 hour.

To make the salmon cakes, in a medium-sized bowl, mix together the salmon, egg, mayonnaise, pork rinds, garlic powder, salt and pepper. Place in the refrigerator to chill for 15 minutes.

Form the salmon mixture into 4 to 6 patties, depending on how big you want them.

Heat a large skillet over medium heat and add the oil. Cook the patties until browned on both sides, about 10 minutes total.

Serve the salmon patties with the aioli. Top with the sliced tomato and avocado if you'd like.

Side Dish Recommendation:
grilled or roasted asparagus

Per serving: Calories: 891.3 kcal | Fat: 78.6 g | Carbs: 3.9 g | Fiber: 0.7 g | Protein: 41.4 g | Net Carbs: 3.2 g

CREAMY CHIPOTLE ASPARAGUS
SCRAMBLED EGGS

I've been making these creamy eggs for years! You'll love the bites of cream cheese with the crunch of the asparagus. It's a great recipe for breakfast, lunch or dinner.

SERVES 3

6 large eggs

1 tbsp (15 ml) water

1 tbsp (14 g) unsalted butter

6 asparagus spears, trimmed and cut into ½" (1.3-cm) pieces

2 oz (56 g) cream cheese, cut into 8 pieces, at room temperature

1 tbsp (15 ml) adobo sauce (from a can of chipotle peppers)

½ tsp coarse salt

¼ tsp freshly ground black pepper

In a medium-sized bowl, beat the eggs with the water until smooth and foamy, about 30 seconds, then set aside.

In a medium-sized skillet, melt the butter over medium-low heat. Add the asparagus and cook, stirring occasionally, for about 2 minutes, or until starting to soften.

Add the beaten eggs to the skillet. Allow the edges to set, then, using a rubber spatula, gently push the edges inward and allow the uncooked eggs to flow to the edge. Don't stir, just gently push it—this is how you get large, fluffy curds of egg.

When the eggs are almost cooked through, dot the top of the eggs with the cream cheese and drizzle with the adobo sauce. Gently stir the cream cheese and sauce into the eggs, just until the eggs are fully cooked and the cream cheese is soft and just starting to melt into the eggs.

Remove the eggs from the heat, season with salt and black pepper and serve.

Side Dish Recommendation:
Cauliflower Rice (page 181)

Per serving: Calories: 263 kcal | Fat: 21.0 g | Carbs: 3.7 g | Fiber: 0.8 g | Protein: 14.5 g | Net Carbs: 2.9 g

GREEK CHICKEN SKEWERS

When it's grilling season, this flavorful chicken is often on our menu. Paired with the creamy tzatziki sauce, it's a wonderfully simple, healthy Keto meal. It's light and lemony with loads of flavor from the herbs!

SERVES 4

FOR THE CHICKEN

½ cup (118 ml) avocado or extra virgin olive oil

1 tsp dried oregano

1 tsp dried rosemary

½ tsp dried thyme

Juice of 2 lemons, plus the zest of 1

3 cloves garlic, minced

2 lb (900 g) boneless, skinless chicken breasts, cut into 1 to 1½" (2.5- to 4-cm) pieces

FOR THE TZATZIKI SAUCE

1 cup (30 g) plain Greek yogurt

1 cup (230 g) sour cream

3 cloves garlic, finely minced or pressed

Juice of ½ lemon

¼ cup (2 g) chopped fresh dill

½ tsp coarse salt

¼ tsp freshly ground black pepper

FOR GRILLING

Oil, for grill

1½ tsp (12 g) coarse salt, divided

½ tsp freshly ground black pepper

2 bell peppers, cut into 1 to 1½" (2.5- to 4-cm) pieces

2 large zucchini, cut into 1 to 1½" (2.5- to 4-cm) pieces

1 tbsp (15 ml) avocado or extra virgin olive oil

To marinate the chicken, in a ziplock bag or a large bowl mix together the avocado oil, oregano, rosemary, thyme, lemon juice and zest and garlic. Add the chicken and shake to coat well. Marinate the mixture in the refrigerator for 1 to 2 hours.

Meanwhile, make the tzatziki sauce. In a bowl, mix together all the sauce ingredients, then cover and place in the fridge until you're ready to eat.

To grill the chicken and vegetables, preheat your grill to 375°F (190°C), usually the medium setting, and lightly oil the grates where you'll be placing your skewers. Remove the chicken from the marinade, discarding the marinade. Season the chicken with 1 teaspoon of the salt and all of the pepper. Toss the vegetables with the avocado oil and season with the remaining salt.

Thread your chicken and vegetables onto 4 metal skewers, then place them on the grates. Cook for about 4 minutes, flip the skewers, then cook another 3 to 4 minutes, or until the chicken is completely cooked through and the veggies are crisp-tender.

Serve with tzatziki sauce for dipping and drizzling.

Side Dish Recommendation:
grilled or roasted asparagus and cherry tomatoes

Per serving: Calories: 443.3 kcal | Fat: 26.8 g | Carbs: 8.1 g | Fiber: 1.3 g | Protein: 39.8 g | Net Carbs: 6.8 g

MEXICAN CHICKEN CAULIFLOWER RICE BOWLS

I like to make a batch of this chicken ahead of time, then assemble my rice bowls when we're ready to eat. The chicken is flavorful enough by itself that you could serve it in a salad or on its own with a side of broccoli. The adobo sauce adds a bit of smoky spice to the marinade, while the lime juice keeps things light and fresh.

SERVES 4

FOR THE MARINADE

Juice and zest of 3 limes

¼ cup (60 ml) avocado or extra virgin olive oil

3 cloves garlic, minced

½ tsp ground cumin

½ tsp onion powder

½ tsp chipotle powder

½ tsp coarse salt

½ tsp freshly ground black pepper

¼ cup (10 g) fresh cilantro, chopped

2 tbsp (30 ml) adobo sauce (from a can of chipotle peppers)

2 lb (900 g) boneless, skinless chicken breasts, cut crosswise into 1" (2.5-cm) slices

FOR THE BOWLS

1 tbsp (15 ml) avocado or extra virgin olive oil

1 bell pepper, sliced

½ medium-sized onion, sliced

2 cloves garlic, minced

6 cups (678 g) cooked Cauliflower Rice (page 181)

¼ cup (56 g) prepared salsa

¼ cup (10 g) chopped fresh cilantro

To make the marinade, in a bowl or ziplock bag combine all the marinade ingredients except the chicken and mix well. Then add the chicken and marinate in the refrigerator for at least 2 hours and up to 4.

Remove the chicken from the marinade when ready to cook; discard the marinade.

Heat a large skillet over medium heat. Add the avocado oil and, when it's shimmering, add the chicken. Cook until lightly browned and cooked through, 6 to 7 minutes. Remove the chicken with a slotted spoon and set aside.

Add the bell pepper and onion to the skillet. Cook, stirring occasionally, just until the onion is soft, about 5 minutes. Add the garlic and cook for 1 minute more. Add the cauliflower rice and cover the pan. Allow the rice to cook for about 3 minutes, or just until tender.

Add the chicken back to the pan and cook for just long enough to heat it. Stir in the salsa and cilantro.

Per serving: Calories: 484.1 kcal | Fat: 26.2 g | Carbs: 8.7 g | Fiber: 2.8 g | Protein: 49.1 g | Net Carbs: 5.9 g

SHRIMP CAKES WITH LEMON-GARLIC AIOLI

This recipe is similar to the Salmon Cakes on page 72, but I think it's slightly more upscale, so this is what I'll serve when friends are over. The creamy lemon and garlic aioli pairs perfectly with the tender shrimp cakes.

SERVES 4

FOR THE AIOLI

¾ cup (174 g) mayonnaise

3 cloves garlic

Juice of 1 lemon

½ tsp coarse salt

2 tbsp (5 g) finely chopped fresh cilantro

FOR THE SHRIMP CAKES

1 lb (454 g) shrimp, peeled, deveined and chopped

¾ cup (72 g) almond flour

2 tbsp (5 g) chopped fresh chives

1 clove garlic, minced

3 tbsp (10 g) finely diced red bell pepper

2 large eggs

1 tsp lemon zest

½ tsp coarse salt

¼ tsp freshly ground black pepper

2 tbsp (30 ml) avocado or extra virgin olive oil

OPTIONAL TOPPINGS

Sliced tomato and/or avocado

To make the aioli, in a small bowl mix together all the aioli ingredients. Cover and refrigerate for at least 1 hour.

To make the shrimp cakes, in a medium-sized bowl combine all the shrimp cake ingredients, except the oil. Form into 6 to 8 patties and place on a plate or sheet pan. Cover and refrigerate for 15 minutes.

Heat a large skillet over medium heat. Add the avocado oil and, when it's shimmering, add the shrimp cakes. Cook the cakes for about 5 minutes per side, or until golden brown and cooked through.

Serve the shrimp cakes with a dollop of aioli, plus sliced tomato and/or avocado if you'd like.

Side Dish Recommendation:
grilled or roasted asparagus

Per serving: Calories: 609.5 kcal | Fat: 49.7 g | Carbs: 7.0 g | Fiber: 2.5 g | Protein: 35.2 g | Net Carbs: 4.5 g

BUFFALO CHICKEN
EGG SALAD BOWLS

Creamy mayonnaise and Buffalo sauce were made for each other! This easy recipe has just a few additional ingredients to take your typical egg salad to an entirely new level. The slight spice of the sauce paired with the creamy blue cheese and crunchy spinach and tomatoes makes this easy lunch or dinner a hit with everyone.

SERVES 4

¼ cup (57 g) mayonnaise

2 tbsp (30 ml) Buffalo Sauce (page 177)

6 hard-boiled large eggs, chopped

1 celery rib, chopped

1 cup (152 g) cooked chicken, chopped

¼ cup (28 g) crumbled blue cheese

½ tsp coarse salt

6 oz (170 g) baby spinach leaves

½ pint (137 g) cherry tomatoes, halved

In a medium-sized bowl, mix together the mayonnaise and Buffalo sauce. Add the eggs, celery and chicken, then mix thoroughly. Add the blue cheese and salt, mixing just until combined. Place in the refrigerator to chill for at least 1 hour, or until you're ready to serve.

Divide the spinach leaves among 4 bowls, then top with the egg salad mixture and tomatoes.

Side Dish Recommendation:
Cauliflower Rice (page 181)

Per serving: Calories: 339.5 kcal | Fat: 25.7 g | Carbs: 3.8 g | Fiber: 1.5 g | Protein: 22.8 g | Net Carbs: 2.4 g

One-Pot
MEALS

If there's one thing I love, it's not having extra dishes to clean. The recipes in this chapter use as few dishes as possible to achieve that goal! I like adding as much flavor as possible—using as few ingredients as possible—to make the cooking process simple and enjoyable. You can see from these recipes that the Keto lifestyle doesn't have to be difficult; you just need some go-to, easy recipes to make it fun!

MY 3 FAVORITES
Mexican Chicken & Cauliflower Casserole (page 102)
Sheet Pan Salsa Chicken & Peppers (page 105)
Creamy Tarragon Chicken & Asparagus (page 106)

MOROCCAN CHICKEN
WITH LEMON & OLIVES

I traveled through Morocco a few years ago and this dish was my absolute favorite. I've re-created it many times, using slightly different ingredients, but this is now the one to which I always return. The salty green olives with the sweet apricots might seem a bit unusual, but once you try it, it will become your favorite, too! I cut back on the amount of dried apricots to keep the carb count low, but it's worth it to keep them in to get that sweet bite!

SERVES 4

3 lb (1.3 kg) skinless chicken thighs

1 tsp coarse salt

1 tsp freshly ground black pepper

1 tbsp (15 ml) avocado or extra virgin olive oil

½ onion, chopped

3 cloves garlic, minced

1 tsp ground cinnamon

½ tsp ground ginger

1 cup (240 ml) chicken broth

½ cup (113 g) sliced green olives

¼ cup (56 g) dried apricots

Juice and zest of 1 lemon

2 tbsp (5 g) chopped fresh parsley

3 cups (339 g) cooked Cauliflower Rice (page 181), for serving

Season the chicken thighs with the salt and pepper. Heat a large skillet over medium heat and add the oil. Working in batches, brown the chicken on both sides, 3 to 4 minutes per side. Remove from the skillet and set aside.

Add the onion to the skillet and cook, stirring occasionally, until soft, about 5 minutes. Add the garlic, cinnamon and ginger. Cook, stirring frequently, for 1 minute more. Remove the pan from the heat.

Add the chicken broth, green olives, apricots, lemon juice and zest to the pan and stir well. Place the chicken in the pan and cover. Cook for 20 to 25 minutes, or until the chicken is almost cooked through. Uncover the pan and keep the sauce at a strong simmer until it thickens and reduces slightly, about 5 minutes. Top with the parsley. Serve over the cauliflower rice.

Per serving: Calories: 480.7 kcal | Fat: 19.5 g | Carbs: 7.8 g | Fiber: 2.2 g | Protein: 64.7 g | Net Carbs: 5.6 g

SKILLET CHICKEN CAPRESE

Caprese salads are a longtime favorite of our family, so I wanted a dish that was more filling but still had those wonderful flavors. This chicken dish is very simple, but it's one I make often because we love it so much.

SERVES 4

2 lb (900 g) boneless, skinless chicken breasts

½ tsp coarse salt

¼ tsp freshly ground black pepper

4 tsp (20 ml) extra virgin olive oil, divided

2 cups (275 g) cherry tomatoes, halved if large

1 head garlic, outer paper removed and cloves separated but not peeled

¼ cup (56 g) Basil Pesto (page 184)

4 slices whole-milk mozzarella

¼ cup (10 g) chopped fresh basil leaves

Preheat your oven to 350°F (176°C).

Season the chicken with the salt and pepper.

Heat a large oven-safe skillet over medium-high heat. Add 2 teaspoons (10 ml) of the olive oil. When it's shimmering, add the chicken breasts. Brown the chicken well on both sides, about 2 minutes per side, then remove the pan from the heat.

Drizzle the tomatoes and garlic with the remaining 2 teaspoons (10 ml) of olive oil, then add them to the skillet. Top each chicken breast with a tablespoon (14 g) of pesto, then a slice of the mozzarella. Bake for 30 minutes, or until the chicken is cooked through.

Squeeze the garlic cloves out of their shells into the skillet. Sprinkle the chicken with the basil leaves and serve.

Side Dish Recommendation:
Creamy Broccoli with Pancetta & Pecorino (page 147)

Per serving: Calories: 606.5 kcal | Fat: 28.2 g | Carbs: 6.8 g | Fiber: 1.6 g | Protein: 77.5 g | Net Carbs: 5.2 g

SPICY SAUSAGE & VEGGIE SAUTÉ

Spicy sausage and fresh, crisp-tender vegetables are even better when they come together in one pan in almost no time flat. I like to add a little salsa and sour cream if I have it on hand, or even an avocado. The point is that this recipe is so versatile yet so flavorful you'll want to make it all the time.

SERVES 4

2 tsp (10 ml) avocado or extra virgin olive oil

1 lb (454 g) spicy sausage, such as andouille, cut into 1" (2.5-cm) pieces

½ cup (76 g) chopped onion

2 cloves garlic, minced

2 cups (226 g) cooked Cauliflower Rice (page 181)

1 red bell pepper, seeded and chopped

1 poblano pepper, seeded and chopped

1 serrano pepper, chopped

1 cup (137 g) cherry tomatoes, halved

1 tsp coarse salt

½ tsp freshly ground black pepper

OPTIONAL TOPPINGS

Salsa, sour cream and/or avocado

In a large skillet, heat the avocado oil over medium heat. Add the sausage and brown well on both sides, stirring occasionally, 5 to 6 minutes. Remove the sausage from the skillet with a slotted spoon and set aside.

Add the onion, garlic, cauliflower rice and the bell, poblano and serrano peppers to the skillet. Cook, stirring occasionally, for about 5 minutes.

Add the sausage back to the pan, along with the cherry tomatoes. Cover and sauté for a few minutes more, or until the veggies are tender but still slightly crisp and the cauliflower rice is cooked through. Season with the salt and black pepper, then serve immediately with your favorite toppings.

Per serving: Calories: 315.3 kcal | Fat: 21.3 g | Carbs: 10.2 g | Fiber: 2.9 g | Protein: 22.1 g | Net Carbs: 7.3 g

---

PEPPER-CRUSTED TENDERLOIN WITH CHARRED BRUSSELS SPROUTS

Yes, the Keto diet can be fancy, too! This delicious wine sauce is so decadent over the tender steaks, and the Brussels sprouts have a nice char that brings it all together.

SERVES 4

4 beef tenderloin steaks (about 2 lb [900 g])

1 tbsp (8 g) coarsely crushed black peppercorns

1 tsp coarse salt

2 tbsp (30 ml) avocado oil

1 lb (454 g) Brussels sprouts, thinly sliced

½ cup (118 ml) Keto-friendly dry red wine, such as cabernet

2 tbsp (28 g) cold, unsalted butter, cut into 2 pieces

Set out the steaks to sit at room temperature for about 30 minutes. Sprinkle with the peppercorns and salt, gently pressing to adhere.

Heat a large skillet over medium-high heat. Add the avocado oil and, when it's shimmering, add half of the sprouts to the pan in one layer. Do not stir for a few minutes, allowing the bottom of the sprouts to char. Remove the first batch and set aside. Repeat with the remaining sprouts. Remove from the pan and set aside.

Add the steaks to the pan. Cook for 4 to 5 minutes per side, or until both sides are well browned and the steaks are cooked to your desired doneness (4 to 5 minutes per side for medium-rare).

Transfer the steaks to a clean cutting board and tent with foil. Add the wine to the pan, stirring to scrape up any browned bits on the bottom. Simmer until the wine is reduced by half, about 5 minutes. Add the butter, 1 piece at a time, stirring until incorporated.

Serve each steak with some of the wine sauce poured over it, with the Brussels sprouts on the side.

Per serving: Calories: 773.2 kcal | Fat: 50.4 g | Carbs: 8.8 g | Fiber: 2.9 g | Protein: 63.6 g | Net Carbs: 5.7 g

OVEN-BAKED CHICKEN THIGHS & ROASTED CAULIFLOWER

This dish is the epitome of the one-pan meal! It all cooks together on one big sheet pan, plus you can have a different flavor chicken thigh for each member of your family if you so choose. We like to have lemon-pepper, barbecue and taco seasonings, but the sky's the limit!

SERVES 4

8 cloves garlic, whole and unpeeled

1 head cauliflower, cut into small florets (about 1 lb [454 g])

2 tbsp (30 ml) avocado or extra virgin olive oil, divided

1 tsp coarse salt, divided

2 lb (900 g) bone-in chicken thighs

Freshly ground black pepper

4 tbsp (57 g) unsalted butter, melted

2 tbsp (16 g) of your favorite seasoning (barbecue, taco [page 178], lemon-pepper [page 179], etc.)

Preheat your oven to 425°F (218°C).

In a bowl, toss the garlic cloves and cauliflower with 1 tablespoon (15 ml) of the avocado oil and ½ teaspoon of the salt, then arrange in a single layer on one side of a large sheet pan. Place the chicken thighs next to the cauliflower on the other side of the sheet pan, then brush with the remaining tablespoon (15 ml) of oil and season with the remaining ½ teaspoon of salt and pepper. It's okay if some of the chicken has to go on top of some of the cauliflower, depending on how large your sheet pan is; alternatively, you can use two sheet pans.

Bake for about 45 minutes, turning the cauliflower halfway through, until the chicken is cooked through to an internal temperature of 165°F (74°C) and the cauliflower is tender.

In a small bowl, mix together the melted butter and seasoning, then brush the mixture over the chicken thighs. Squeeze the garlic out of its paper shells and discard the shells. Gently mix the roasted garlic with the cauliflower (don't worry if there are chunks anywhere; it's very mellow and delicious). Serve immediately.

Per serving: Calories: 617.8 kcal | Fat: 44.9 g | Carbs: 10.6 g | Fiber: 5.3 g | Protein: 43.4 g | Net Carbs: 5.3 g

STUFFED PORK LOIN & ASPARAGUS

This dish looks so pretty sliced and served alongside the asparagus. And don't let the "stuffed" part of this dish scare you away, as the bacon makes it easy to keep the blue cheese nicely tucked inside. Use a high-quality balsamic glaze, available now at most grocery stores.

SERVES 4

1 tbsp + 1 tsp (20 ml) avocado or extra virgin olive oil, divided

1 lb (454 g) pork loin

½ cup (56 g) crumbled blue cheese

8 slices bacon (not thick cut)

¼ cup (60 ml) balsamic glaze, divided (check bottle to make sure there's no added sugar)

1 lb (454 g) asparagus, trimmed

½ tsp coarse salt

Preheat your oven to 400°F (204°C).

Heat an oven-safe skillet over medium heat. Add 1 tablespoon (15 ml) of the avocado oil and, when it's shimmering, add the pork loin. Cook until browned on all sides, about 6 minutes. Remove the loin from the pan and place on a cutting board.

Cut a large slit lengthwise into the pork loin, taking care not to cut all the way through. Stuff with the blue cheese and hold it closed.

Lay the bacon on a large cutting board with the edges slightly overlapping lengthwise. Set the pork loin on the bacon. Slowly roll up the pork loin and bacon until the pork loin is completely covered.

Place the pork loin on an oven-safe rack set on a sheet pan. You can cover the sheet pan with aluminum foil, if desired, for easy cleanup later. Brush 2 tablespoons (30 ml) of the balsamic glaze over the bacon. Bake for 20 minutes.

Meanwhile, on a plate, toss the asparagus with the remaining teaspoon of avocado oil and the salt, then set aside.

Brush the bacon with the remaining 2 tablespoons (30 ml) of balsamic glaze, then return the pork loin to the oven, adding the asparagus around it, and bake for another 5 minutes, or until the pork loin is cooked through and the asparagus is crisp-tender.

Remove from the oven and allow the pork to rest for 10 minutes, then slice and serve.

Per serving: Calories: 454.8 kcal | Fat: 25.7 g | Carbs: 9.3 g | Fiber: 2.4 g | Protein: 44.4 g | Net Carbs: 6.9 g

ROASTED LEMON-ROSEMARY CHICKEN & CAULIFLOWER

The sauce in this chicken dish is absolutely to die for. The lemon and rosemary combine with the rendered fat from the thighs that is wonderful with the cauliflower once it's all baked together. And the garlic softens, so you can eat that as is or smear it on the top of your chicken.

SERVES 4

¼ cup (60 ml) avocado or extra virgin olive oil

Juice and zest of 1 lemon

2 tbsp (28 g) capers

2 tbsp (5 g) fresh rosemary, chopped

2 lb (900 g) bone-in chicken thighs

1 tsp coarse salt

½ tsp freshly ground black pepper

1 head cauliflower, broken into florets

8 cloves garlic, peeled and lightly crushed

Preheat your oven to 425°F (218°C).

In a bowl, mix together the avocado oil, lemon juice and zest, capers and rosemary. Set it aside.

Season the chicken with the salt and pepper. Place the chicken, cauliflower and garlic in a 9 x 13–inch (23 x 33–cm) baking dish, in one layer, if possible. Top with the sauce.

Bake for 50 to 60 minutes, or until the chicken is cooked through to an internal temperature of 165°F (74°C) and the cauliflower is soft.

Per serving: Calories: 715.7 kcal | Fat: 44.4 g | Carbs: 9.2 g | Fiber: 3.8 g | Protein: 66.7 g | Net Carbs: 5.4 g

CAJUN JUMBO SHRIMP & SAUSAGE SKILLET

It's amazing how a small amount of spice can turn just a few ingredients into a flavor powerhouse. Shrimp are extremely low in carbs, making them the perfect choice for this flavorful Keto dish.

SERVES 4

1 tbsp (15 ml) avocado or extra virgin olive oil, plus more for skillet

2 lb (900 g) jumbo shrimp, peeled and deveined

2 large zucchini, sliced

2 red bell peppers, seeded and sliced

1 lb (454 g) andouille sausage, sliced

1 tbsp (8 g) Cajun Seasoning (page 180)

In a large bowl, combine 1 tablespoon (15 ml) of the avocado oil with the shrimp, zucchini and bell peppers. Toss to coat.

Heat a large skillet over medium-high heat. Add the oil and, when it's shimmering, add the sausage. Cook until the sausage is starting to brown, about 5 minutes.

Add the shrimp mixture and Cajun seasoning to the skillet and cook until the shrimp is cooked through and the zucchini and peppers are starting to soften, about 5 more minutes.

Side Dish Recommendation:
Cauliflower Rice (page 181)

Per serving: Calories: 343 kcal | Fat: 13.0 g | Carbs: 6.8 g | Fiber: 2.1 g | Protein: 51.2 g | Net Carbs: 4.7 g

MEXICAN CHICKEN & CAULIFLOWER CASSEROLE

Everyone needs a good casserole recipe in their repertoire, and Keto-lovers are no exception. This family-friendly meal is hot and cheesy, just like a good casserole should be.

SERVES 4

1 tbsp (15 ml) avocado or extra virgin olive oil

1 medium-sized onion, chopped

3 cloves garlic, minced

1 tsp ground cumin

1 pint (300 g) cherry tomatoes

1 (14.5-oz [411-g]) can fire-roasted diced tomatoes

1 (4-oz [113-g]) can diced green chiles

4 cups (452 g) cooked Cauliflower Rice (page 181)

4 cups (560 g) shredded rotisserie chicken

2 cups (224 g) shredded Mexican-blend cheese

Preheat your oven to 350°F (176°C).

In a large, oven-safe skillet, heat the avocado oil over medium heat. When the oil is shimmering, add the onion and cook, stirring occasionally, until it begins to soften, 4 to 5 minutes. Add the garlic and cumin and cook, stirring frequently for another minute. Remove the pan from the heat.

Add the cherry tomatoes, fire-roasted tomatoes, chiles, cauliflower rice and shredded chicken to the pan, stirring well. Flatten the top a bit with your spoon or spatula so it's even, then sprinkle the shredded cheese over the top.

Bake for about 30 minutes, or until hot and bubbling and the cheese is lightly browned.

Per serving: Calories: 326.7 kcal | Fat: 19.2 g | Carbs: 8.6 g | Fiber: 2.9 g | Protein: 28.0 g | Net Carbs: 5.7 g

SHEET PAN SALSA
CHICKEN & PEPPERS

If you haven't tried making Keto sheet pan meals yet, this is a great one to start with. It comes together extra quickly with the aid of prepared salsa, yet it's healthy and delicious. Its Mexican flavors are kid friendly, but adults will love it, too.

SERVES 4

4 boneless, skinless chicken breasts (about 2 lb [900 g])

1 tbsp (8 g) Taco Seasoning (page 178)

2 red bell peppers, seeded and sliced

2 poblano peppers, seeded and sliced

½ large red onion, chopped

2 tbsp (30 ml) extra virgin olive oil

⅓ cup (75 g) prepared salsa

½ cup (56 g) shredded Mexican-blend cheese

¼ cup (10 g) chopped fresh cilantro

¼ cup (58 g) sour cream

Preheat your oven to 400°F (204°C).

Place the chicken breasts on a large sheet pan. Sprinkle evenly with the taco seasoning.

Place the bell peppers, poblanos and red onion around the chicken on the sheet pan. Drizzle chicken and vegetables with the olive oil. Top the chicken evenly with the salsa.

Bake for 30 minutes, or until the chicken is almost completely cooked through. Top with the shredded cheese and continue to bake for 3 to 5 minutes longer, or until the cheese is melted and the chicken is thoroughly cooked to an internal temperature of 165°F (74°C).

Remove from the oven and sprinkle the chicken with the cilantro. Place 1 chicken breast and some veggies on each of 4 serving plates. Add a dollop of sour cream and enjoy.

Per serving: Calories: 386.8 kcal | Fat: 16.3 g | Carbs: 6.9 g | Fiber: 1.5 g | Protein: 50.3 g | Net Carbs: 5.4 g

---

CREAMY TARRAGON CHICKEN & ASPARAGUS

Tarragon is one of my favorite herbs but you don't see it often enough in recipes, in my opinion. It adds such a wonderful flavor to this easy dish, plus the creamy sauce and the protein from the chicken make this a great Keto dinner. The asparagus really brings all the flavors together into a meal your family will love!

SERVES 4

4 boneless, skinless chicken breasts, sliced crosswise into ½" (1.3-cm) pieces

1½ tsp (12 g) coarse salt, divided

¼ tsp freshly ground black pepper

1 tbsp (15 ml) avocado or extra virgin olive oil

8 oz (225 g) asparagus, trimmed and cut into ½" (1.3-cm) slices

¾ cup (180 ml) heavy cream

4 tsp (20 ml) Dijon mustard

1 tbsp (3 g) chopped fresh tarragon

Season the chicken breasts with 1 teaspoon of the salt and pepper. Heat the avocado oil in a large skillet over medium heat and, when shimmering, add the chicken. Cook until the chicken is browned and cooked through, to an internal temperature of 165°F (74°C), about 8 minutes. Remove from the pan and set aside.

Add the asparagus to the pan and sauté for 2 minutes. Add the cream and Dijon and stir to combine. Add the chicken back to the pan along with the tarragon. Simmer for a few more minutes, until it's slightly thickened and the asparagus is cooked to crisp-tender. Add the remaining ½ teaspoon salt.

Per serving: Calories: 594.4 kcal | Fat: 30.2 g | Carbs: 4.0 g | Fiber: 1.4 g | Protein: 73.0 g | Net Carbs: 2.6 g

CAJUN SHRIMP & CAULIFLOWER
"GRITS"

Shrimp and grits has always been one of my favorite meals. Cauliflower rice makes a great substitute for the grits, and the sauce is so heavenly that you'll never notice the difference! The tender shrimp paired with the flavorful, creamy sauce makes this dish one you'll make again and again.

SERVES 4

1 lb (454 g) large shrimp, peeled and deveined

1 tbsp (8 g) Cajun Seasoning (page 180), divided

1 tsp coarse salt, divided

2 tsp (10 ml) avocado or extra virgin olive oil

½ green bell pepper, seeded and chopped

4 cups (452 g) cooked Cauliflower Rice (page 181)

½ medium-sized tomato, chopped

½ cup (118 ml) heavy cream

2 tbsp (5 g) chopped fresh parsley

Season the shrimp with 1 teaspoon of the Cajun seasoning and ½ teaspoon of the salt, then set aside.

Heat a large skillet over medium heat. Add the avocado oil and, when it's shimmering, add the shrimp. Cook the shrimp, tossing them occasionally, until they're just cooked through, 3 to 4 minutes. Remove the shrimp from the pan and set aside.

Add the bell pepper and cauliflower rice to the pan and cook for a few minutes, until they start to soften. Add the tomato, cream, the remaining ½ teaspoon of salt and the remaining 2 teaspoons (6 g) of Cajun seasoning, stir well, then cook for about 2 minutes, or until the tomatoes are soft and the sauce is starting to thicken.

Divide the "grits" among 4 bowls and top with the shrimp and parsley.

Per serving: Calories: 336.9 kcal | Fat: 21.2 g | Carbs: 6.3 g | Fiber: 2.4 g | Protein: 30.4 g | Net Carbs: 3.9 g

Scrumptious
SOUPS & SALADS

Having plenty of Keto meals at the ready makes the Keto lifestyle not just enjoyable, but simple, too! Soups and salads are two staples that make that happen almost effortlessly. Make a big pot of soup, then enjoy those leftovers throughout the week, especially because many soups taste even better the next day.

For quick yet delicious and satisfying lunches or dinners, I make sure to keep plenty of fresh spinach in the fridge as well as a container of homemade dressing. Chicken & Spinach Salad with Parmesan Dressing (page 112) is a great example of how you can put together a terrific meal in a snap, because the shredded chicken, spinach, hard-boiled eggs, cooked bacon and dressing can all be kept prepped ahead of time and then assembled whenever hunger hits. You'll find many salads in this chapter that you can mix and match, all by keeping some Keto staple ingredients prepped and at the ready!

MY 3 FAVORITES
Chicken & Spinach Salad with Parmesan Dressing (page 112)
Cauliflower Cheese Soup with Pancetta (page 116)
Chicken, Bacon & Blue Cheese Broccoli Salad (page 124)

CHICKEN & SPINACH SALAD WITH PARMESAN DRESSING

If there's one green salad I'd call our favorite, it's this one. It's perfect for Keto because you get protein from the chicken but the mayo-based dressing is pretty high in fat. I make a big batch of the dressing, then shred the meat from a rotisserie chicken and keep it in the fridge so we can whip these up whenever someone is hungry. Even my girls go nuts over this one!

SERVES 2

FOR THE DRESSING

1½ cups (345 g) mayonnaise

¼ cup (60 ml) fresh lemon juice

1 tbsp (15 ml) Dijon mustard

1 tsp Tabasco sauce

1 tsp coconut aminos (or soy sauce, but it's not as Keto-friendly)

½ tsp coarse salt

½ tsp freshly ground black pepper

1 cup (180 g) grated Parmesan cheese

FOR THE SALAD

3 oz (85 g) baby spinach leaves

1 cup (8 oz [227 g]) shredded rotisserie chicken

¼ cup (46 g) halved cherry tomatoes

¼ cup (46 g) sliced baby cucumber

To make the dressing, in a small bowl mix together all the dressing ingredients, except the Parmesan cheese. Then, add the Parmesan and mix well. Store in a container in the refrigerator until you're ready to make the salad.

To make the salad, in a large bowl assemble the salad ingredients and top with 2 tablespoons (30 ml) of the dressing.

Gently toss to coat the salad in the dressing and serve. Store extra dressing in the fridge.

FOR THE DRESSING
Per serving (2 tbsp [30 ml]): Calories: 103.4 kcal | Fat: 10.7 g | Carbs: 0.4 g | Fiber: 0 g | Protein: 1.4 g | Net Carbs: 0.4 g

FOR THE SALAD
Per serving: Calories: 249.2 kcal | Fat: 9.2 g | Carbs: 2.8 g | Fiber: 1.4 g | Protein: 36.8 g | Net Carbs: 1.4 g

---

CREAMY CHICKEN & POBLANO SOUP

This hearty soup is filling enough that everyone will be happy after dinner. It's creamy and rich with a lot of flavor. I'll serve it on the side with any one of the Mexican dishes in this book or as a main dish with a side of fresh vegetables.

SERVES 4

4 poblano peppers

2 tbsp (28 g) unsalted butter or ghee

½ cup (76 g) chopped red onion

3 cloves garlic, minced

2¼ cups (540 ml) chicken broth

1 cup (112 g) shredded Mexican-blend cheese

8 oz (225 g) cream cheese, at room temperature, cut into 12 pieces

¼ cup (60 ml) heavy cream

3 cups (420 g) cooked, shredded chicken

1 tsp coarse salt

½ tsp freshly ground black pepper

¼ cup (28 g) crumbled queso fresco

¼ cup (10 g) chopped fresh cilantro

Place the poblano peppers over a gas flame, or on a sheet pan under the broiler on HIGH, until they're blackened, turning them over to ensure most spots are black. Transfer them to a ziplock bag and allow them to sit for at least 10 minutes, or until they're cool enough to handle. Using your hands, remove the skins from the peppers, then the stems and seeds. Chop the peppers and set them aside.

In a large saucepan or stockpot, melt the butter over medium heat. Add the red onion and cook, stirring occasionally, until it begins to soften, 4 to 5 minutes. Add the garlic and cook, stirring frequently, for another minute.

Pour the chicken broth into the pot and add the peppers. Simmer for about 10 minutes, then carefully use an immersion blender to puree the soup until it's very smooth.

Add the shredded cheese and cream cheese, stirring until well incorporated and smooth. Add the cream, shredded chicken, salt and black pepper. Stir well.

Spoon into 4 bowls and top each with a small amount of queso fresco and chopped cilantro.

Per serving: Calories: 556.3 kcal | Fat: 38.0 g | Carbs: 6.8 g | Fiber: 0.9 g | Protein: 46.1 g | Net Carbs: 5.9 g

CAULIFLOWER CHEESE SOUP WITH PANCETTA

If everything is better with bacon, then it's even better with pancetta! It adds a wonderful salty flavor to this soup. Perfect for the cold weather months or just when you have a craving for it. And you will crave it, I promise you!

SERVES 4

8 oz (225 g) pancetta, chopped

½ medium onion, chopped

1 clove garlic, minced

1 large head cauliflower, cut into florets (about 1 lb [454 g])

4½ cups (1 L) unsalted chicken broth

2 cups (224 g) shredded cheddar cheese

4 oz (112 g) cream cheese, at room temperature, cut into 8 pieces

⅓ cup (80 ml) heavy cream

1 tsp coarse salt

½ tsp freshly ground black pepper

In a large saucepan or stockpot, cook the pancetta over medium heat until crisp, about 8 minutes. Remove the pancetta with a slotted spoon and set aside, leaving the fat in the pot.

Add the onion and cook, stirring occasionally, until it begins to soften, 4 to 5 minutes. Add the garlic and cook, stirring frequently, for another minute.

Add the cauliflower, then pour in the chicken broth. Bring to a boil, then lower the heat to medium-low and simmer until the cauliflower is tender, about 30 minutes.

Using an immersion blender, puree the soup until it's very smooth. Stir in the cheddar and cream cheese, stirring until well incorporated and smooth. Add the cream, salt and pepper and stir well.

Ladle into 4 bowls and top each with some of the reserved pancetta.

Per serving: Calories: 347.4 kcal | Fat: 28.9 g | Carbs: 6.1 g | Fiber: 1.7 g | Protein: 16.0 g | Net Carbs: 4.3 g

---

CHILLED AVOCADO & CRAB SOUP

I love making soups because they're so simple and made all in one pot. But chilled soups aren't as easy to come by, and I miss them in the summer months. This creamy, elegant soup is incredibly simple—you just need a blender!—and it's perfect for a filling lunch or dinner.

SERVES 4

3 large, ripe avocados

¼ cup (58 g) sour cream

3 cups (708 ml) chicken broth

Juice of 1 lime

¼ cup + 2 tbsp (15 g) chopped fresh cilantro, divided

1 tsp ground cumin

1 tsp coarse salt

8 oz (225 g) fresh crabmeat

In a high-powered blender, combine the avocados, sour cream, broth, lime juice, ¼ cup (10 g) of the cilantro, cumin and salt. Blend until very smooth. Transfer to a lidded container and place the soup in the refrigerator to thoroughly chill, about 3 hours.

Ladle the soup into 4 bowls and top each with a quarter of the crabmeat and a sprinkle of the remaining 2 tablespoons (5 g) of cilantro. Serve immediately.

Per serving: Calories: 193.5 kcal | Fat: 14.1 g | Carbs: 7.6 g | Fiber: 4.8 g | Protein: 11.9 g | Net Carbs: 2.8 g

WEDGE SALAD WITH
BACON, BLUE CHEESE & BALSAMIC

This is the salad I make whenever we have a dinner party or a holiday meal. It's fast and easy and can be made ahead of time, then assembled just before serving. People who aren't on the Keto diet don't even mind that it's Keto—it's just delicious!

SERVES 4

FOR THE DRESSING

¾ cup (174 g) mayonnaise

¼ cup (58 g) sour cream

½ cup (118 ml) heavy cream

1 cup (112 g) crumbled blue cheese

Juice of ½ lemon

Dash of Worcestershire sauce

½ tsp coarse salt

½ tsp freshly ground black pepper

FOR THE BALSAMIC REDUCTION

¾ cup (180 ml) balsamic vinegar

FOR THE SALAD

1 head iceberg lettuce, cored and cut into 4 wedges

10 slices bacon, cooked and crumbled

½ pint (89 g) cherry tomatoes, quartered

To make the dressing, in a small bowl, mix together all the dressing ingredients and store in the refrigerator until ready to use.

To make the balsamic reduction, in a small saucepan bring the vinegar to a boil. Lower the heat and keep at a strong simmer until reduced by about one-third and the mixture coats a spoon, 4 to 5 minutes.

Remove from the heat and let cool (the reduction will thicken as it cools). If it's too thick, add a bit more vinegar: Place back over low heat and stir until incorporated. If it's not thick enough, put back on the burner until it thickens a bit more. Set aside while you assemble the salads.

To assemble the salad, place each lettuce wedge on a serving plate. Top with the dressing, balsamic reduction, crumbled bacon and cherry tomatoes.

Per serving: Calories: 363 kcal | Fat: 32.1 g | Carbs: 6.9 g | Fiber: 1.0 g | Protein: 11.5 g | Net Carbs: 5.9 g

STEAK SALAD WITH CILANTRO-JALAPEÑO PESTO

Using pesto as a salad dressing is one of my favorite Keto secrets. This pesto uses cilantro instead of basil and has some jalapeños for a little spice and depth of flavor. Keep this one in mind for those occasions when you have leftover steak, too!

SERVES 4

FOR THE CILANTRO-JALAPEÑO PESTO

5 jalapeño peppers

4 cloves garlic

1 bunch cilantro (4–5 cups [160–200 g])

1 cup (185 g) pine nuts

Juice of 1 lime

½ cup (90 g) Parmesan cheese

¾ cup (180 ml) avocado oil or extra virgin olive oil

½ tsp coarse salt

¼ tsp freshly ground black pepper

FOR THE STEAKS

1 tbsp (15 ml) avocado oil (or another oil with a high smoke point, such as canola)

2 rib-eye steaks (about 1 lb [454 g]), at room temperature

1 tsp coarse salt

1 tsp freshly ground black pepper

FOR THE SALAD

6 oz (170 g) baby spinach leaves

1 red bell pepper, seeded and chopped

1 cucumber, chopped

1 cup (137 g) cherry tomatoes, halved

To make the pesto, place the jalapeños on a sheet pan under the broiler on HIGH until they're blackened in spots, turning them over to ensure they're blackened on all sides, 7 to 8 minutes. Remove from the oven and allow them to cool. Slice off the stems and set aside.

In a high-powered blender, combine all the pesto ingredients, including the roasted jalapeños, and blend until smooth. Allow the pesto to sit at room temperature while you make the steaks, to allow the flavors to meld.

To make the steaks, heat a 12-inch (30-cm) cast-iron skillet over high heat until very hot, 5 to 6 minutes.

Brush the rib eyes with the avocado oil, then season both sides of the steaks with the salt and black pepper.

Place the steaks in the hot skillet (you may have to work in batches; don't crowd the pan). Cook for 3 to 4 minutes, then flip the steaks and cook for another 3 minutes, or until they reach an internal temperature of 140°F (60°C) for medium-rare, or 155°F (68°C) for medium.

Transfer the steaks to a cutting board and let them rest for 5 minutes. Slice the steaks against the grain and set aside.

To assemble the salad, place the spinach leaves in a large serving bowl. Add the sliced steak, bell pepper, cucumber and cherry tomatoes. Top with ½ cup (118 ml) of the pesto "dressing" and gently toss to coat. Serve with more pesto on the side.

Note: This pesto is great just with the steaks and a side dish, too! It's also delicious tossed with roasted cauliflower.

Per serving: Calories: 1006.7 kcal | Fat: 93.9 g | Carbs: 11.1 g | Fiber: 3.3 g | Protein: 27.5 g | Net Carbs: 7.8 g

CHICKEN, BACON & BLUE CHEESE BROCCOLI SALAD

This salad has a lot of history around our house. My daughter, Kylie, started asking me when I was going to make "salade" again (even she doesn't know why she started calling it that). Then everyone started calling it that, so that's what it is to us now. You'll just call it SO GOOD! I will double the batch and it will still be gone within a day. It keeps well, tastes amazing and is the perfect Keto food.

SERVES 6

2 lb (900 g) broccoli

1¼ cups (287 g) mayonnaise

2 tbsp (30 ml) apple cider vinegar

¾ cup (84 g) shredded cheddar cheese

1 rotisserie chicken (4–5 cups [560–700 g]), meat removed and shredded

1 lb (454 g) bacon, cooked and crumbled

½ medium-sized red onion, chopped

1 cup (112 g) crumbled blue cheese

1½ tsp (12 g) coarse salt

½ tsp freshly ground black pepper

Using a food processor, shred the broccoli until very fine, then transfer to a large bowl.

In a small bowl, stir together the mayonnaise and vinegar.

Add the mayonnaise mixture to the broccoli and stir well. Mix in the cheddar cheese, chicken, bacon, red onion, blue cheese, salt and pepper until well incorporated. Refrigerate until ready to serve.

Per serving: Calories: 583.5 kcal | Fat: 44.1 g | Carbs: 6.7 g | Fiber: 2.1 g | Protein: 42.7 g | Net Carbs: 4.6 g

LEMON CHICKEN & SPINACH SOUP

I make so many versions of this soup, even I can't recall them all. Sometimes I use zucchini noodles, sometimes cauliflower rice and sometimes spinach. The egg yolks make it creamy and luscious without the added fat, which is good if you've already hit your fat macros for the day. Of course, you can always add a bit of heavy cream if you're looking for a fat boost!

SERVES 6

¼ cup (57 g) unsalted butter

1 lb (454 g) boneless, skinless chicken breasts, cut into bite-size pieces

½ medium-sized onion, chopped

1 celery rib, chopped

½ tsp dried oregano

5 cups (1.2 L) chicken broth

½ cup (118 ml) fresh lemon juice

6 large egg yolks

6 oz (170 g) fresh spinach

1 tsp coarse salt

½ tsp freshly ground black pepper

In a stockpot, melt the butter over medium heat. Add the chicken and cook until lightly browned on all sides, about 5 minutes. Remove the chicken with a slotted spoon and set aside.

Add the onion, celery and oregano to the pot and sauté for about 5 minutes, or until the onion is soft.

Return the chicken to the pot, then pour in the chicken broth. Simmer for 20 minutes.

In a medium-sized bowl, beat together the lemon juice and egg yolks. Slowly stir in 2 cups (480 ml) of the hot broth, whisking continuously (this is called tempering). Pour the egg mixture into the pot, stirring well.

Add the spinach and stir just until it's wilted. Season with the salt and pepper and serve.

Per serving: Calories: 319.3 kcal | Fat: 19.0 g | Carbs: 4.8 g | Fiber: 1.0 g | Protein: 31.5 g | Net Carbs: 3.8 g

CHARRED BRUSSELS SPROUTS SALAD WITH BACON & BALSAMIC-DIJON VINAIGRETTE

Adding a nice char to Brussels sprouts transforms them into a vegetable that even the haters will love. The dressing and crispy bacon make them even more scrumptious, and it pairs well with the earthy sprouts.

SERVES 4

FOR THE DRESSING

2 tbsp (30 ml) balsamic vinegar

2 tsp (10 ml) Dijon mustard

1 clove garlic, minced

¼ cup (60 ml) avocado or extra virgin olive oil

Pinch of coarse salt

Pinch of freshly ground black pepper

FOR THE SPROUTS

6 slices bacon, cut crosswise into ½" (1.3-cm) pieces

1 lb (454 g) Brussels sprouts, trimmed and thinly sliced

To make the dressing, in a small bowl whisk together the balsamic vinegar, Dijon and garlic. Slowly stream in the avocado oil, whisking constantly until thoroughly combined. Set aside while you make the Brussels sprouts.

To make the sprouts, heat a large skillet over medium-high heat. Cook the bacon until crispy, 8 to 10 minutes. Remove the bacon with a slotted spoon and set aside, leaving the bacon fat in the skillet.

Add half of the sprouts to the pan so they're in one layer. Do not stir for a few minutes, allowing the bottom of the sprouts to char. Remove and set aside. Repeat with the remaining sprouts.

Place the sprouts in a serving dish along with the reserved bacon. Toss with the dressing, salt and pepper and serve.

Per serving: Calories: 498.9 kcal | Fat: 49.3 g | Carbs: 6.7 g | Fiber: 2.1 g | Protein: 4.7 g | Net Carbs: 4.6 g

---

ROASTED BROCCOLI CHEESE SOUP

Roasting your broccoli is the key to an amazing broccoli cheese soup. The slightly browned bits add a wonderful depth of flavor, yet this recipe is still very simple.

SERVES 4

1 large head broccoli, cut into small to medium-sized florets

¼ cup (60 ml) avocado or extra virgin olive oil, divided

1 tsp coarse salt, divided

½ medium-sized sweet onion, chopped

2 cups (480 ml) low-sodium chicken broth

1½ cups (360 ml) heavy cream

2 cups (224 g) shredded sharp cheddar cheese

½ tsp freshly ground black pepper

Preheat your oven to 400°F (204°C).

Place the broccoli on a sheet pan. Drizzle with 2 tablespoons (30 ml) of the avocado oil, then season with ½ teaspoon of the salt and toss well. Place in the oven and roast until browned, about 20 minutes or so. Remove from the oven and set aside.

Meanwhile, in a large soup pot, heat the remaining 2 tablespoons (30 ml) of oil. Add the onion and sauté until soft and translucent, about 5 minutes. Pour in the chicken broth. Simmer until hot, about 2 minutes.

Add the cream and broccoli. Using an immersion blender, blend the soup until thick and fairly smooth. Heat the mixture just until very hot (do not boil). Stir in the cheddar cheese until melted and incorporated fully. Season with the remaining ½ teaspoon of salt and the pepper.

Per serving: Calories: 621.9 kcal | Fat: 61.0 g | Carbs: 7.0 g | Fiber: 2.0 g | Protein: 10.5 g | Net Carbs: 5.0 g

CREAMY TACO SOUP

This easy soup is perfect for Keto because there's plenty of protein from the beef, and the sauce is creamy and rich from the cream cheese. The fire-roasted tomatoes add a wonderful flavor, but feel free to use regular diced tomatoes if that's all you have on hand.

SERVES 4

1 tsp avocado or extra virgin olive oil

½ medium-sized onion, chopped

1 lb (454 g) ground beef

2 tbsp (16 g) Taco Seasoning (page 178)

1 (14.5-oz [411-g]) can fire-roasted diced tomatoes, undrained

1 (4-oz [113-g]) can diced green chiles, undrained

3 cups (708 ml) chicken broth

8 oz (226 g) cream cheese, at room temperature, cut into 8 pieces

½ tsp coarse salt

¼ tsp freshly ground black pepper

OPTIONAL TOPPINGS

Sour cream

Shredded cheddar cheese

Chopped green onion

Heat a large pot or Dutch oven over medium heat. Add the avocado oil and, when it's shimmering, add the onion. Cook, stirring occasionally, for about 2 minutes. Add the ground beef and cook, stirring occasionally, until almost no pink remains, 7 to 8 minutes. Drain off the fat.

Add the taco seasoning and stir well. Add the fire-roasted tomatoes and diced chiles with their juices, plus the chicken broth. Stir well and bring to a boil. Lower the heat and simmer, stirring occasionally, for 15 minutes. Add the cream cheese to the pot, stirring until it's incorporated. Season with the salt and pepper and serve with your desired toppings.

Per serving: Calories: 268.7 kcal | Fat: 17.9 g | Carbs: 6.5 g | Fiber: 1.5 g | Protein: 19.6 g | Net Carbs: 5.0 g

Tasty & Tempting
SIDE DISHES

Side dishes were something I often overlooked when I first began the Keto lifestyle. I somehow just forgot about them and focused on getting in the groove with main dishes. There are so many great Keto sides to make, however, and I've included my favorites here. A few are even hearty enough to enjoy as a meal! They all pair well with the recipes in this book, making them great weeknight choices.

MY 3 FAVORITES
Twice-Baked Mashed Parmesan Cauliflower (page 139)
Green Beans Almondine (page 143)
Bacon-Wrapped Brussels Sprouts with Maple Syrup (page 144)

MUSHROOM & CAULIFLOWER
RISOTTO

I don't know anyone who doesn't love a good risotto, and I'm not sure I could be completely Keto without this recipe. It's the perfect accompaniment to the Pepper-Crusted Tenderloins (page 93), or just serve it alongside a nice salad.

SERVES 6

2 tbsp (28 g) unsalted butter

2 tbsp (30 ml) avocado or extra virgin olive oil

1 lb (454 g) cremini mushrooms, sliced

1 large shallot, minced

2 cloves garlic, minced

1 large head cauliflower, riced (about 4 cups [650 g])

½ cup (118 ml) heavy cream

1 cup (180 g) grated Parmesan cheese

½ tsp coarse salt

½ tsp freshly ground black pepper

Heat a large skillet over medium-high heat. Melt the butter in the skillet, then add the avocado oil and mushrooms. Cook the mushrooms, stirring occasionally, until they've released their liquid and it's evaporated, and they're starting to brown, about 8 minutes. Add the shallot, garlic and cauliflower to the pan and cook, stirring frequently, for 3 minutes more.

Add the cream and Parmesan cheese to the pan. Cook for about another 5 minutes, or until the cauliflower is cooked through and the sauce is hot and bubbling. Season with the salt and pepper and serve.

Per serving: Calories: 167.4 kcal | Fat: 13.8 g | Carbs: 7.7 g | Fiber: 2.5 g | Protein: 5.1 g | Net Carbs: 5.2 g

TWICE-BAKED MASHED PARMESAN CAULIFLOWER

Steaming the cauliflower until soft, mashing it until it's smooth as silk, then baking it with a buttery Parmesan topping makes this cauliflower dish worthy of your fanciest dinner parties! Yet it's still simple enough that you'll be making it for your weeknight meals, too. It's creamy and luscious—I'm constantly being asked for the recipe whenever someone new tries it. The secret is the addition of the egg yolks. And, of course, the buttery Parmesan topping adds wonderful flavor, too!

SERVES 8

8 cups cauliflower florets (about 3 lb [1.3 kg])

6 tbsp (84 g) unsalted butter, at room temperature, divided

3 large egg yolks

⅓ cup (80 ml) heavy cream

2 tsp (16 g) coarse salt

Cooking spray

½ cup (90 g) grated Parmesan cheese

Place the cauliflower in a steamer basket set inside a pot above boiling water, then cover the pot. Steam until the cauliflower is very tender, 8 to 10 minutes. Remove the cauliflower from the pot and allow it to cool until cool enough to handle.

Preheat your oven to 375°F (190°C).

Place your cauliflower in a large mixing bowl. Add 2 tablespoons (27 g) of the butter, plus the egg yolks and the cream. Using an immersion blender, puree the cauliflower until smooth. Alternatively, you can use a potato masher if you like a chunkier consistency. Add the salt and stir well to incorporate.

Spray an 11 x 7-inch (28 x 18-cm) baking dish with cooking spray. Pour the cauliflower puree into the prepared baking dish, spreading it out evenly.

Melt the remaining 4 tablespoons (57 g) of butter in a small bowl in the microwave. Stir in the Parmesan cheese. Pour the mixture over the cauliflower puree, then gently spread it over the top.

Bake for 30 minutes, or until lightly browned on the top and bubbling slightly at the sides.

Per serving: Calories: 132.3 kcal | Fat: 11.1 g | Carbs: 5.6 g | Fiber: 2.6 g | Protein: 4.2 g | Net Carbs: 2.9 g

STUFFED ZUCCHINI WITH GOAT CHEESE & MARINARA

I usually don't bother with stuffing zucchini, opting instead for sautéing the ingredients for the sake of ease of preparation. But this recipe is the exception. The creamy goat cheese is a nice contrast to the slight crunch of the zucchini.

SERVES 8

4 medium-sized zucchini

1 tsp avocado or extra virgin olive oil

½ tsp coarse salt

¼ tsp freshly ground black pepper

4 oz (113 g) goat cheese, at room temperature, divided

1 cup (240 ml) Marinara Sauce (page 183)

¼ cup (10 g) chopped fresh parsley

Preheat your oven or grill to 400°F (204°C).

Slice the zucchini in half lengthwise and scoop out the seeds, leaving the zucchini hollowed out. Brush the avocado oil onto the outside of the zucchini. Season the zucchini with salt and pepper. If cooking in the oven, place the zucchini halves, hollowed side up, on a baking sheet.

Using half of the goat cheese, spread a small amount in the hollow of each zucchini half. Spoon the marinara sauce on top, then dot with the remaining goat cheese.

Bake or grill until the goat cheese is soft and the marinara is bubbling, about 10 minutes. Sprinkle with parsley and serve immediately.

Per serving: Calories: 77.6 kcal | Fat: 5.6 g | Carbs: 3.8 g | Fiber: 1.4 g | Protein: 3.9 g | Net Carbs: 2.4 g

---

GREEN BEANS ALMONDINE

Welcome to your go-to, super simple Keto side dish! There is almost never a time I don't have green beans on my shopping list because everyone devours this dish so fast. Even the leftovers are delicious!

SERVES 4

1 lb (454 g) green beans, trimmed

¼ cup (57 g) unsalted butter

½ cup (55 g) slivered almonds

Juice of ½ lemon

½ tsp coarse salt, or to taste

In a large skillet, bring 1 cup (240 ml) of water to a boil. Add the green beans and cover for 4 to 5 minutes, just until they're crisp-tender. Drain the beans in a colander and set aside.

Melt the butter in the same skillet. Add your almonds and sauté them for a few minutes until they start to brown.

Return the green beans to the skillet and toss to coat them with your buttery almonds. Squeeze the lemon juice over the green beans. Season with the salt.

Per serving: Calories: 151.8 kcal | Fat: 12.9 g | Carbs: 8.2 g | Fiber: 3.8 g | Protein: 3.5 g | Net Carbs: 4.4 g

BACON-WRAPPED BRUSSELS SPROUTS WITH MAPLE SYRUP

Brussels sprouts haters, I'm here to change your mind. This 3-ingredient recipe is perfect for a party or just a snack. The crispy bacon gets a syrupy coating from the Keto maple syrup that is just to die for!

SERVES 4

1 lb (454 g) Brussels sprouts, trimmed and halved

1 lb (454 g) bacon, cut crosswise into thirds

½ cup (120 ml) Keto-friendly pure maple syrup (such as Lakanto), plus more for serving

Preheat your oven to 400°F (204°C).

Wrap each Brussels sprout half with a piece of bacon. Place, seam side down, on an oven-safe rack set on a sheet pan (a broiler pan works well, too). Brush with some of the maple syrup.

Bake for 20 minutes, or until the bacon is starting to get crispy. Brush with more maple syrup and continue to bake for another 10 minutes, or until the bacon is crispy and the Brussels sprouts are cooked through.

Serve with extra maple syrup.

Per serving: Calories: 422.4 kcal | Fat: 26.9 g | Carbs: 30.3 g |
Fiber: 11.8 g | Protein: 27.6 g | Sugar Alcohols: 11.9 g | Net Carbs: 6.6 g

CREAMY BROCCOLI
WITH PANCETTA & PECORINO

I love cooked broccoli, but this recipe really transforms it into something special. Pancetta brings so much flavor, and the creamy sauce is rich and luscious. Even your kids will thank you for being Keto with this one!

SERVES 6

8 oz (225 g) pancetta, cut into cubes

¼ medium-sized onion, chopped

2 cloves garlic, minced

1 head broccoli, broken into small florets

1 cup (240 ml) heavy cream

¼ cup (28 g) shredded mozzarella cheese

½ cup (90 g) grated pecorino

Preheat your oven to 400°F (204°C).

Heat a large, oven-safe skillet over medium heat. Add the pancetta and cook until almost crispy, about 7 minutes. Add the onion and cook for 2 minutes, then add the garlic and cook, stirring frequently, for 1 more minute.

Add the broccoli, cream, mozzarella and pecorino to the pan, then toss gently to coat. Bake the broccoli for about 15 minutes, or until cooked through.

Per serving: Calories: 327.8 kcal | Fat: 28.9 g | Carbs: 7.4 g | Fiber: 2.6 g | Protein: 10.1 g | Net Carbs: 4.8 g

CHIPOTLE CAULIFLOWER
"POTATO" SALAD

I've been making a version of this recipe for years, but had to modify it when I began eating Keto. I was pleasantly surprised at how well the cauliflower stands in for the potatoes! The flavors are nicely balanced, and it has a smoky spiciness from the chipotle peppers. It's the perfect side dish for a weeknight meal or a summer barbecue!

SERVES 6

4 cups (1.3 kg) cauliflower florets

1 tbsp (15 ml) avocado or extra virgin olive oil

1 cup (230 g) mayonnaise

3 chipotle peppers from a can of chipotles in adobo sauce, minced

2 tbsp (5 g) fresh cilantro

2 green onions, chopped

¼ cup (45 g) seeded and chopped red bell pepper

1 celery rib, chopped

8 oz (225 g) bacon, cooked and crumbled

4 hard-boiled large eggs, coarsely chopped

½ tsp coarse salt

¼ tsp freshly ground black pepper

Preheat your oven to 425°F (218°C).

On a sheet pan, toss the cauliflower florets with the avocado oil.

Roast in the oven, tossing the florets at the 20-minute point, for 30 to 40 minutes, until crisp-tender and slightly caramelized.

In a small bowl, mix together the mayonnaise, chipotle peppers and cilantro.

In a separate bowl, combine the green onions, bell pepper, celery, bacon, eggs and roasted cauliflower, then add the mayonnaise mixture. Stir gently to combine. Season with the salt and black pepper.

Refrigerate for at least 1 hour before serving.

Per serving: Calories: 277.8 kcal | Fat: 19.5 g | Carbs: 6.4 g | Fiber: 3.1 g | Protein: 18.7 g | Net Carbs: 3.3 g

BACON BROCCOLI CHEESE BITES

These easy, cheesy bites are what I make for my girls when they come home after a big test day because they're always starving! They're also great as an appetizer or a side dish. If I'm making them as part of a main course, I like to serve them alongside some grilled chicken.

SERVES 2

2 cups (454 g) cooked broccoli florets, finely chopped

2 large eggs

2 tbsp (16 g) finely minced red onion

1 clove garlic, minced

½ cup (48 g) almond flour

1 cup (112 g) shredded cheddar cheese

3 slices bacon, cooked and finely chopped

½ tsp coarse salt

¼ tsp finely ground black pepper

Preheat your oven to 400°F (204°C).

In a large bowl, mix together the broccoli, eggs, red onion and garlic until thoroughly combined. Stir in the almond flour, then the cheddar cheese, bacon, salt and pepper.

Drop by tablespoons onto a baking sheet lined with parchment paper, then form each into a smooth ball. Bake the bites for about 30 minutes, or until lightly browned.

Per serving: Calories: 234.4 kcal | Fat: 16.8 g | Carbs: 9.9 g | Fiber: 4.2 g | Protein: 13.2 g | Net Carbs: 5.7 g

CHIPOTLE & SAUSAGE
DEVILED EGGS

Adding a bit of smoky adobo sauce to your deviled eggs is divine, but when you bite into them and find a sausage surprise, it's even better! Use your favorite sausage flavor in this recipe—they're all delicious!

SERVES 8

2 tsp (10 ml) extra virgin olive oil

8 oz (225 g) andouille sausage, diced

12 hard-boiled large eggs

⅓ cup (76 g) mayonnaise

2 tbsp (30 g) sour cream

1 tbsp (15 ml) adobo sauce (from a can of chipotle peppers in adobo sauce)

½ tsp coarse salt

In a large skillet, heat the olive oil over medium-high heat. When the oil is shimmering, add the diced sausage and cook until lightly browned, 5 to 6 minutes.

Slice the eggs in half lengthwise and remove the yolks. In a medium-sized bowl, mix together the yolks, mayo, sour cream, adobo sauce and salt until very smooth, using a fork to vigorously break up the yolks, if necessary.

Place the egg whites on a platter and divide the diced sausage equally among the hollowed-out eggs. Then, pipe or spoon the yolk filling into the eggs.

Cover and refrigerate until ready to serve.

Per serving: Calories: 246.1 kcal | Fat: 19.9 g | Carbs: 1.5 g | Fiber: 0.1 g | Protein: 14.6 g | Net Carbs: 1.4 g

RAJAS CON CREMA
(POBLANOS IN CREAM)

If ever you were looking for a great side dish to your Mexican meal, this is it. It's creamy and rich with a slight spice from the poblanos, making it a good complement to chicken or steak, too.

SERVES 4

1 tbsp (15 ml) avocado or extra virgin olive oil

1 medium-sized white onion, sliced

1 clove garlic, minced

4 poblano peppers, roasted and peeled

¾ cup (180 ml) heavy cream

½ tsp coarse salt

¼ tsp freshly ground black pepper

Heat a skillet over medium heat. Add the avocado oil and, when it's shimmering, add the onion. Cook until soft and translucent, about 5 minutes. Add the garlic and cook for 1 more minute, stirring frequently.

Add the poblano peppers and cream to the skillet. Simmer for a few minutes, or until the cream and peppers are hot. Season with the salt and black pepper.

Per serving: Calories: 113.1 kcal | Fat: 10.3 g | Carbs: 5.0 g | Fiber: 1.2 g | Protein: 1.3 g | Net Carbs: 3.8 g

BACON JAM

If you've never had bacon jam, then you're in for a real treat. This jam is perfect on just about everything—try it on top of burgers or an avocado, or add a dollop to a salad or vegetables. The coffee in this recipe adds a nice depth of flavor, but you won't even notice it in the final dish!

2 lb (900 g) bacon, sliced crosswise into ½" (1.3-cm) pieces

1 medium-sized sweet onion, chopped

3 cloves garlic, smashed and peeled

½ cup (118 ml) brewed strong coffee

½ cup (118 ml) apple cider vinegar

½ cup (64 g) Keto-friendly light brown sugar (such as Swerve)

¼ cup (60 ml) Keto-friendly pure maple syrup (such as Lakanto)

In a large skillet, cook the bacon over medium heat until crispy, 7 to 8 minutes. Drain off most of the fat (leave just enough to coat the pan), then add the onion to the pan. Cook the onion, stirring occasionally, until it begins to soften, 4 to 5 minutes. Add the garlic and cook, stirring frequently, for another minute.

Stir in the coffee, vinegar, brown sugar and maple syrup. Lower the heat to low and simmer, stirring occasionally, for about 1 hour, or until the mixture has thickened.

Pour the mixture into a high-powered food processor and pulse it a few times, until it's spreadable but still a bit chunky.

Per serving: Calories: 366.2 kcal | Fat: 26.5 g | Carbs: 4.5 g | Fiber: 1.0 g | Protein: 25.8 g | Sugar Alcohols: 1.1 g | Net Carbs: 2.4 g

Sweet KETO BITES

Everyone needs a sweet treat now and then! I'm not a sweets girl, but even I get my cravings occasionally. These desserts are all different enough that you can make them often and not grow tired of them, and they all taste just like their originals! They're also simple enough that they can easily be made on a weeknight. The Chocolate Chip Cookies (page 160) are better than any other I've had, and the Panna Cotta with Fresh Berries (page 171) is a delightful treat for a dinner party. Try them all and decide for yourself!

MY 3 FAVORITES

Chocolate Chip Cookies (page 160)
Salted Peanut Butter Cookie Dough Fat Bombs (page 164)
Chocolate Mousse (page 167)

CHOCOLATE CHIP COOKIES

I'm not exaggerating when I say that these are our favorite chocolate chip cookies, Keto or otherwise. I swear you won't know they're not the real thing! Although they have a few unusual ingredients you may not be used to, please do give them a try. You will be *so* glad you did!

SERVES 8

¾ cup (171 g) unsalted butter, at room temperature

½ cup (100 g) granulated erythritol (such as Swerve)

1 large egg

1 tsp pure vanilla extract

2 tbsp (12 g) coconut flour

1¼ cups (120 g) almond flour

1 tbsp (8 g) arrowroot powder

½ tsp xanthan gum

½ tsp baking soda

1 tsp salt

½ cup (92 g) Keto-friendly chocolate chips (such as Lily's)

Preheat your oven to 350°F (176°C).

In a large bowl, cream the butter and erythritol until very smooth and almost fluffy (this takes a couple of minutes). Add the egg and vanilla, mixing until incorporated, 20 to 30 seconds.

In a medium-sized bowl, whisk together the coconut flour, almond flour, arrowroot powder, xanthan gum, baking soda and salt.

Mix half of the flour mixture into the butter mixture, taking care not to overmix. Once it's just incorporated, add the rest of your flour mixture and again mix just until it's fully incorporated. Stir in the chocolate chips.

Drop the cookie dough in 1-inch (2.5-cm) portions about 2 inches (5 cm) apart onto an ungreased sheet pan, then bake for 10 to 12 minutes, or until the cookies are lightly browned and baked through. The baking time will largely depend on the size of your cookies.

Store in an airtight container for 3 to 4 days, or in the refrigerator for up to a week. These Keto cookies can also be frozen for up to 3 months.

Per serving: Calories: 311.2 kcal | Fat: 29.8 g | Carbs: 21.2 g | Fiber: 4.7 g | Protein: 5.2 g | Sugar Alcohols: 12.9 g | Net Carbs: 3.6 g

CHOCOLATE MERINGUES

I like to keep these meringues around for when I need just a small bite of something sweet to get me through the day. They're also great on a cookie tray during the holidays!

SERVES 6

3 large egg whites, at room temperature

⅛ tsp cream of tartar

½ tsp pure vanilla extract

½ cup (100 g) granulated erythritol (such as Swerve)

2 tbsp (16 g) Dutch-processed cocoa powder

Preheat your oven to 300°F (148°C). Line a sheet pan with parchment paper.

In a medium-sized bowl, beat the egg whites until foamy. Add the cream of tartar and vanilla, then continue to beat until soft peaks form. Beat in the erythritol, a little at a time, until stiff peaks form. Gently fold in the cocoa powder, being careful not to overmix.

Drop a teaspoon at a time onto the prepared sheet pan. Bake for about 30 minutes, or just until the tops begin to harden. Remove from the oven and allow the meringues to cool on the pan completely before enjoying.

Per serving: Calories: 22 kcal | Fat: 0.3 g | Carbs: 17.2 g | Fiber: 0.7 g | Protein: 2.2 g | Sugar Alcohols: 16.0 g | Net Carbs: 0.5 g

SALTED PEANUT BUTTER
COOKIE DOUGH FAT BOMBS

If you love raw cookie dough, then these are the treat for you. The creamy peanut butter with the salty chocolate will make you so glad you're part of the Keto clan!

SERVES 6

FOR THE COOKIE DOUGH

1 cup (96 g) almond flour

½ cup (48 g) coconut flour

½ cup (62 g) powdered erythritol (such as Swerve)

Pinch of coarse salt

½ cup (113 g) peanut butter or almond butter

¼ cup (60 ml) coconut oil, melted but not hot

1 tsp pure vanilla extract

FOR THE CHOCOLATE TOPPING

½ cup (92 g) Keto-friendly chocolate chips (such as Lily's)

1 tsp coconut oil

½ tsp flaky sea salt

In a medium-sized bowl, whisk together the almond and coconut flours, erythritol and salt. Stir in the peanut butter, coconut oil and vanilla until a dough forms.

Line a sheet pan with parchment paper. Using a 1-inch (2.5-cm) cookie scoop, divide the dough into balls. Place them in the freezer for 10 to 15 minutes.

To make the chocolate topping, just before removing the cookie dough bites from the freezer, microwave the chocolate chips and coconut oil in 30-second increments until almost melted. Stir until melted and smooth. (Mine takes about 1 minute total, then I stir vigorously until completely melted.)

Spoon the chocolate evenly over the cookie dough bites. Once they're almost set, sprinkle with sea salt. Store in the refrigerator.

Per serving: Calories: 249.7 kcal | Fat: 22.6 g | Carbs: 17.6 g | Fiber: 6.3 g | Protein: 5.4 g | Sugar Alcohols: 7.7 g | Net Carbs: 3.6 g

CHOCOLATE MOUSSE

Chocolate mousse is one of those desserts I'll always order if it's on the menu at dinner. It's so simple to make at home, too, and this version is entirely Keto-friendly! Add a few fresh raspberries if you'd like.

SERVES 2

3 oz (85 g) cream cheese, at room temperature

½ cup (118 ml) heavy cream

2 tbsp (16 g) Dutch-processed cocoa powder

⅓ cup (42 g) powdered erythritol (such as Swerve)

½ tsp pure vanilla extract

¼ tsp coarse salt

In a bowl, beat together the cream cheese and cream until smooth. Add the cocoa powder and erythritol and beat again until smooth. Stir in the vanilla and salt.

Refrigerate for at least 1 hour.

Per serving: Calories: 370.3 kcal | Fat: 36.1 g | Carbs: 28.1 g | Fiber: 0 g | Protein: 4.3 g | Sugar Alcohols: 24.0 g | Net Carbs: 4.1 g

LEMON & RASPBERRY NO-BAKE
CHEESECAKE JARS

This light and creamy cheesecake filling has just a few ingredients but will keep your sweet side satisfied. I've even been known to sneak a spoonful out of the fridge when I need a pick-me-up.

SERVES 8

2 (8-oz [226-g]) packages cream cheese, at room temperature

½ cup (62 g) powdered erythritol (such as Swerve)

½ cup (118 ml) heavy cream

Juice and zest of 1 lemon

Pinch of salt

½ cup (76 g) fresh raspberries

In a medium-sized bowl, beat together the cream cheese and erythritol with a mixer or by hand until smooth. Add the cream, lemon juice and zest and the salt and beat until fully incorporated. Chill the mixture for at least 1 hour.

Divide the mixture among 8 jars or bowls. Top with the fresh raspberries and serve.

Per serving: Calories: 260.7 kcal | Fat: 25.0 g | Carbs: 14.0 g | Fiber: 0.6 g | Protein: 4.0 g | Sugar Alcohols: 9.0 g | Net Carbs: 4.4 g

PANNA COTTA WITH FRESH BERRIES

Panna cotta is one of those recipes that is elegant and impressive enough to serve to company but so simple you can treat yourself anytime! It does need some chill time, so if making this for an ending to a weeknight meal, just be sure to make it the night before or even that morning.

SERVES 8

4 cups (960 ml) heavy cream

½ cup (100 g) granulated erythritol (such as Swerve)

1 vanilla bean, split lengthwise and seeds scraped from pod, or 2 tsp (10 ml) pure vanilla extract

2 (½-oz [14-g]) packets plain powdered gelatin

6 tbsp (90 ml) cold water

½ cup (76 g) fresh raspberries or blueberries

In a saucepan, heat the cream, erythritol and vanilla over medium-low heat, stirring occasionally, until the erythritol is dissolved.

In a small bowl, sprinkle the gelatin over the cold water and let stand for at least 5 minutes.

Stir the gelatin into the warm cream mixture until completely dissolved.

Pour into 8 dessert molds, cover lightly and chill until very firm, at least 4 hours.

Top each with fresh berries and serve.

Per serving: Calories: 424 kcal | Fat: 43.0 g | Carbs: 16.3 g | Fiber: 0.5 g | Protein: 5.0 g | Sugar Alcohols: 12.0 g | Net Carbs: 3.8 g

---

PEANUT BUTTER PIE FAT BOMBS

I have always been a huge fan of peanut butter pie. It's creamy and decadent—so much so that I have to refrain from eating it all in one sitting! To combat that, I started making it bite-size and keeping it in the freezer for a sweet treat at a moment's notice. And if you're making it on a weeknight, it's delicious right out of the bowl, too!

SERVES 6

6 oz (170 g) cream cheese, at room temperature

½ cup (62 g) powdered erythritol (such as Swerve)

½ cup (125 g) creamy peanut butter

½ tsp pure vanilla extract

¾ cup (180 ml) heavy whipping cream, chilled

Line a sheet pan with parchment paper.

In a medium-sized bowl, beat together the cream cheese, erythritol and peanut butter until smooth. Stir in the vanilla.

In a separate medium-sized bowl, whip the cream until stiff peaks form. Fold the whipped cream into the peanut butter mixture just until combined.

Using a 1-inch (2.5-cm) cookie scoop, place scoops of the mixture on the prepared sheet pan. Place in the freezer for 1 hour or until they're firm, then remove from the pan and transfer to a ziplock bag. Store in the freezer.

Per serving: Calories: 253.5 kcal | Fat: 23.7 g | Carbs: 14.4 g | Fiber: 0.8 g | Protein: 5.5 g | Sugar Alcohols: 9.0 g | Net Carbs: 4.6 g

---

Pantry STAPLES

One of the frustrating things about starting Keto is that we may not realize some foods we take for granted are higher in carbs. I created recipes for some common ones so that I could control the ingredients and, therefore, the carbs. All of these staples are used in some of the recipes in this book and, if I've tried and like a similar product, I've included the brand name in case you'd prefer to just pick up a ranch dressing, for instance, instead of making one. But I encourage you to give these a try—they're delicious and work wonderfully with your Keto lifestyle!

MY 3 FAVORITES

Cajun Seasoning (page 180)
Cauliflower Rice (page 181)
Basil Pesto (page 184)

RANCH DRESSING

We're big fans of ranch dressing around here, and it's perfect for the Keto diet. Use it as a dip for Keto-friendly veggies, such as celery, cucumbers or cauliflower. Use it on burgers, on your salads or as a sauce to chicken wings, such as the Lemon-Pepper Chicken Wings (page 61). However you choose to use it, the fresh flavor of this homemade dressing will win you over!

MAKES 2 CUPS (480 ML)

In a bowl or Mason jar, mix all the ingredients together. Refrigerate for at least 2 hours to allow the flavors to meld.

1 cup (240 ml) avocado or olive oil mayonnaise

½ cup (115 g) full-fat sour cream

1 clove garlic, minced

Juice of ½ lemon

1 tsp dried chives

1 tsp dried dill

½ tsp onion powder

¼ cup (10 g) chopped flat-leaf parsley leaves, or 2 tsp (2 g) dried

½ tsp coarse salt

¼ tsp freshly ground black pepper

Note: Regular mayonnaise can be used; however, it's thicker and the end result may need a little water to thin it out to your desired consistency.

Store-bought Substitute I Love:
Primal Kitchen

Per serving (2½ tbsp [38 ml]): Calories: 145.5 kcal | Fat: 15.6 g | Carbs: 1 g | Fiber: 0.1 g | Protein: 0.5 g | Net Carbs: 0.9 g

BUFFALO SAUCE

As a lover of all things spicy, Buffalo sauce is right up my alley. My sister Jolie and I have been making a version of this sauce for years, mixing equal parts of cayenne pepper sauce with melted butter for our chicken wings. A few years ago, I decided to add just a few more ingredients that, in my humble opinion, make it that much better. Try this recipe in anything that calls for Buffalo sauce, or just pour some over a fresh avocado for a light lunch or snack.

MAKES 1½ CUPS (360 ML)

1 cup (240 ml) cayenne pepper sauce (such as Frank's RedHot)

½ cup (114 g [1 stick]) unsalted butter, preferably grass-fed

1 tbsp (15 ml) white vinegar

Pinch of garlic powder

½ tsp coarse salt

In a medium-sized saucepan, combine the pepper sauce and butter and heat over medium heat, stirring occasionally, until the butter is melted and the mixture is hot, about 5 minutes. Stir in the vinegar, garlic powder and salt.

You can serve immediately, tossed with cooked wings or used in your favorite recipes. It keeps well in the refrigerator for up to a month; stir well before reusing.

Store-bought Substitute I Love:
The New Primal

Per serving (3 tbsp [45 ml]): Calories: 101.9 kcal | Fat: 11.5 g | Carbs: 0 g | Fiber: 0 g | Protein: 0.7 g | Net Carbs: 0 g

TACO SEASONING

If I could choose my last meal, it would include Mexican flavors. Because I'm such a fan, I like to make my own taco seasoning that suits my family's tastes. This version has a medium spice level with loads of flavor. Try it in the recipes in this book that call for it, or in any of your own Keto favorites.

MAKES ½ CUP (21 G)

In a bowl, mix all the ingredients together, then store in a tightly sealed jar until you are ready to use it.

¼ cup (32 g) chili powder

1 tsp garlic powder

1 tsp onion powder

1 tsp oregano

1 tsp paprika

1 tsp smoked paprika (or another tsp of regular paprika)

2½ tsp (8 g) ground cumin

½ tsp cayenne powder

2 tsp (5 g) coarse salt

1½ tsp (4 g) freshly ground black pepper

Store-bought Substitute I Love:
Primal Palate

Per serving (1 tbsp [2.6 g]): Calories: 19.3 kcal | Fat: 0.8 g | Carbs: 3.5 g | Fiber: 1.9 g | Protein: 0.9 g | Net Carbs: 1.6 g

LEMON-PEPPER SEASONING

I'm addicted to drying lemon peel for this easy seasoning. I'll buy a big bag, zest it all while I'm chatting with the kids or listening to an audiobook, then make a double or triple batch. You can also mix the zest with some erythritol for a Keto-friendly lemon sugar or just with the salt for a lemon salt that's delicious sprinkled on fish and chicken. But my favorite is, hands down, this Lemon-Pepper Seasoning. Use it to make the Lemon-Pepper Chicken Wings (page 61) that are so simple but so delicious, it will become one of your favorite recipes!

MAKES ¼ CUP (50 G)

5 large lemons

¼ cup (40 g) peppercorns

2 tsp (5 g) coarse salt

Preheat your oven to its lowest setting.

Using a paring knife or vegetable peeler, remove just the outer yellow peel from the lemon, taking care to leave as much of the white pith behind as possible.

Line a sheet pan with parchment paper, then spread the strips of lemon peel on the pan in one layer. Place in the oven and allow the lemon peel strips to dry out, 2 to 3 hours. Be sure to check on them and remove them as soon as they're completely dried out.

In a spice grinder or a high-powered blender, combine the dried lemon and peppercorns and process until mostly smooth but the peppercorns still have a few coarse pieces. Mix in the salt and pour into a small, airtight jar for storage.

Store-bought Substitute I Love:

McCormick, Spiceology

Per serving (2 tsp [8 g]): Calories: 13.9 kcal | Fat: 0.2 g | Carbs: 3.7 g | Fiber: 1.7 g | Protein: 0.6 g | Net Carbs: 2.1 g

CAJUN SEASONING

Cajun flavors are one of my favorites, so it follows that I'd have a jar of Cajun seasoning on hand at all times. Cajun Chicken Alfredo (page 41) works perfectly with this homemade seasoning as it's just spicy enough to please everyone. Feel free to add more or less cayenne pepper to make it the perfect level for you and your family.

MAKES ⅓ CUP (77 G)

2 tbsp (16 g) paprika

2 tbsp (16 g) garlic powder

1 tbsp (8 g) onion powder

1 tbsp (8 g) Italian seasoning

1 tbsp (8 g) freshly ground black pepper

1 tbsp (8 g) cayenne pepper

1 tbsp (8 g) coarse salt

2 tsp (5 g) dried thyme

In a bowl, mix all the ingredients together, then store in a tightly sealed jar until you're ready to use it.

Store-bought Substitute I Love:

Spiceology, Frontier

Per serving (2 tsp [10 g]): Calories: 21.7 kcal | Fat: 0.4 g | Carbs: 4.7 g | Fiber: 1.6 g | Protein: 1.0 g | Net Carbs: 3.1 g

CAULIFLOWER RICE

Cauliflower rice is so simple to make and can be enjoyed as is, tossed with some pesto or your favorite seasonings or used in numerous recipes. I like to make several batches of the uncooked rice, freeze it in individual portions, then prepare it as needed. You can start the cooking process with the frozen rice; just add a couple of minutes to the cooking time.

MAKES 4 CUPS (452 G)

1 head cauliflower, broken into florets

1 tbsp (15 ml) avocado or extra virgin olive oil

½ tsp coarse salt

¼ tsp freshly ground black pepper

Fit a food processor with a grating blade, then process the florets into "rice."

Heat a large skillet over medium heat, then add the avocado oil and cauliflower rice, stirring to combine. Cover and cook for 6 to 7 minutes, or until the rice is cooked to your liking.

Season with the salt and pepper.

Store-bought Substitutes I Love:
Trader Joe's, Costco

Per serving (1 cup [113 g]): Calories: 60.6 kcal | Fat: 4.0 g | Carbs: 5.1 g | Fiber: 2.9 g | Protein: 2.3 g | Net Carbs: 2.2 g

TOMATO SAUCE

This simple recipe is intended to mimic the typical canned tomato sauce available in most grocery stores. It's best to use in recipes that call for canned tomato sauce versus using as a stand-alone sauce to serve over pasta. It only takes a minute to make and you can keep the ingredients on hand for any time you need it!

1 (28-oz [794-g]) can San Marzano peeled tomatoes

¼ cup (60 ml) extra-virgin olive oil

1 tsp garlic powder

½ tsp onion powder

½ tsp coarse salt

¼ tsp freshly ground black pepper

In a high-powered blender, combine all the ingredients and blend until smooth.

Store-bought Substitutes I Love:
This recipe is so simple that I've never had a need to purchase a store-bought version!

Per serving (7 tbsp [105 ml]): Calories: 81.8 kcal | Fat: 6.8 g | Carbs: 4.5 g | Fiber: 1.7 g | Protein: 0.9 g | Net Carbs: 2.8 g

MARINARA SAUCE

The need for a good marinara sauce cannot be understated. It's simple but should have enough flavor that there's no need for any additions. The onions and garlic add the perfect amount of flavor to complement the tomatoes, and the crushed red pepper adds that extra something without much spice. I don't suggest using anything but San Marzano tomatoes as they have the best flavor and will make your marinara something really special.

MAKES 5 CUPS (1.2 L)

¼ cup (60 ml) extra virgin olive oil

½ small onion, chopped

5 garlic cloves, thinly sliced

1 (28-oz [794-g]) can San Marzano peeled tomatoes

½ cup (118 ml) water

2 fresh basil sprigs

Pinch of crushed red pepper flakes

1 tsp coarse salt

¼ tsp freshly ground black pepper

In a large skillet, heat the olive oil over medium heat. When it's shimmering, add the onion and cook, stirring occasionally, until it starts to soften, 4 to 5 minutes. Add the garlic and cook for another minute, stirring frequently.

Add the tomatoes, crushing each tomato with your hands before dropping it in the skillet. Add the water and basil. Simmer, uncovered, until the sauce has thickened, about 30 minutes.

Stir in the red pepper flakes, salt and black pepper. If you prefer a smoother sauce, use an immersion blender until the sauce reaches your desired consistency.

Store-bought Substitute I Love:
Rao's

Per serving (½ cup plus 2 tbsp [150 ml]): Calories: 86.7 kcal | Fat: 6.8 g | Carbs: 5.7 g | Fiber: 1.8 g | Protein: 0.9 g | Net Carbs: 3.9 g

BASIL PESTO

I adore basil pesto and grow a huge basil plant in my yard each summer just for this purpose. I cut back on the pine nuts since starting Keto, but the recipe is just as delicious now as then. Use this easy recipe when called for in this book, or try some over an avocado, on scrambled eggs, with a bite or two of a good cheese or mixed into some cauliflower rice.

MAKES 3½ CUPS (285 G)

2 cups (40 g) lightly packed fresh basil

¼ cup (35 g) pine nuts

2 cloves garlic

⅔ cup (160 ml) extra virgin olive oil

½ tsp kosher salt

½ tsp freshly ground black pepper

¾ cup (135 g) shredded Parmesan cheese

In a food processor or high-powered blender, combine all the ingredients except the Parmesan cheese. Blend on high speed until very smooth. Add the Parmesan and blend again until smooth.

Store-bought Substitute I Love:
DeLallo

Per serving (½ cup plus 1 tbsp [47 g]): Calories: 308.6 kcal | Fat: 31.5 g | Carbs: 1.7 g | Fiber: 0.3 g | Protein: 6.1 g | Net Carbs: 1.4 g

ACKNOWLEDGMENTS

Rob Wadsworth, for being my taste tester, listening ear and never-ending inspiration. We do Keto pretty darn well together (just like we do everything). You're the absolute best, kehd. My life is so much better with you in it!

My parents, Joyce and Art Heppner, for being the best two people I've ever known. I'm so proud of the kind, hardworking, funny and loving people you are. I am so grateful for you and I love you to the moon and back!

My girls, Kylie and Katie, for making me laugh every day! You're both such wonderful, nice girls who continuously make me one proud mom.

Lara Nesbit, my best girlfriend and practically a sister. Thanks for keeping me laughing throughout this process and for always being an inspiration!

The team at Page Street Publishing, who continues to believe in me and has brought my career to a whole new level. I am so grateful and proud to be one of your authors.

Special shout-out to my editor, Sarah Monroe, who always has the right answers. You trust me enough to let me run with things, forgive me when I falter and are endlessly supportive. You're amazing!

ABOUT THE AUTHOR

KRISTY BERNARDO is mostly self-taught when it comes to cooking, but she has also been strongly influenced by her mother and grandmother. She honed her skills at the Culinary Institute of America in Hyde Park, New York, and has owned a successful business as a personal chef. She's taught cooking classes to all ages, speaks at conferences and events and has appeared regularly on video and television. Her work as both a food and travel writer has appeared in many mainstream online publications, such as *Huffington Post*, *Food & Wine* magazine, *Better Homes & Gardens* and many more.

Kristy started her Keto lifestyle in June 2018 and was immediately hooked. She spent months creating new recipes for herself and her family, focusing on recipes that use traditional ingredients that were fast and delicious. After her first two books, *Weeknight Cooking with your Instant Pot®* and *Cooking from Frozen with your Instant Pot®*, were published, creating another book that focused on easy, weeknight Keto meals was a natural progression.

Kristy lives in northern Virginia with her two daughters, Kylie and Katie; her partner, Rob; their two cats, Mr. Pepper and Princess Whiskers; and their often naughty but always loveable dog Molly. You can most often find her walking the nearby trails, riding her motorcycle in Virginia's gorgeous wine country or trying new dishes and cocktails at restaurants everywhere.

INDEX